VANISHING EAGLES

VANISHING EAGLES

ILLUSTRATED BY TREVOR BOYER

WRITTEN BY PHILIP BURTON

DODD, MEAD & COMPANY
NEW YORK

First published in the United States of America in 1983
by Dodd, Mead & Company, Inc.
79 Madison Avenue, New York, N.Y. 10016
by arrangement with Dragon's World Ltd
Illustrations copyright © 1981:
color plates, Eagle Star Ins. Co. Ltd;
support illustrations, Trevor Boyer
through Linden Artists Ltd; habitat drawings,
Michael Long, Daleguild Ltd
Text copyright © 1983 Dragon's World Ltd

Library of Congress Cataloging in Publication Data

Boyer, Trevor.
  Vanishing eagles.

  1. Eagles.   I. Burton, Philip John Kennedy.
II. title.
QL696.F32B69   1983   598′.916   83-1900
ISBN 0-396-08168-1

Printed in Spain

AUTHOR'S NOTE

No book on eagles could be written without paying tribute to the achievements of the late Leslie Brown, who, until his recent death, had done more than almost any single person to further knowledge and appreciation of birds of prey in general, and eagles in particular.

Had he lived longer, he would certainly have been involved with this project, but as it is we owe him a great debt not only for a wealth of factual information but for the enthusiasm which all his writings are able to inspire.

If this volume can in its turn kindle a lifelong interest in eagles among some of those who read it, we shall have repaid our debt in the way he would most have wished.

Philip Burton

CONTENTS

FOREWORD

Artists and writers have found inspiration in the beauty and power of eagles while shepherds, farmers and gamekeepers have seen them as enemies, to be destroyed at every opportunity. The romantic image purveyed by the former has at times been nearly as biased and in-accurate as the catalog of supposed crimes laid at their door by the latter.

Either way, humanity has been little help to the birds until recently, and throughout the world, their numbers and ranges have continued to dwindle, so that many are now among the world's most threatened birds.

The urgent need now is for knowledge and understanding to replace the bigoted attitudes of the past. This beautiful book will surely play an important part in furthering this aim.

A superb series of paintings have been married to an informative and readable text to produce a work which will inspire both admiration and concern for these splendid birds.

John Parslow
DIRECTOR
CONSERVATION
Royal Society for the
Protection of Birds

13

INTRODUCTION

The title of this book requires some explanation. All eagles could be described as "vanishing". Like nearly all birds of prey, they are threatened by persecution, habitat loss and pollution. In making this selection we have tried to include the most endangered species but at the same time to portray the diversity of eagles throughout the world. It does not follow that only these 30 are dwindling, or that eagles not on the list have a secure future.

Even more explanation is needed for the word "eagle" itself. Like many other common names for birds, it does not refer to any scientifically recognized group, and the nearest we can approach to a simple definition is to say that eagles are large hawks, but even the word "hawk" varies in its application! The situation can be summarized as follows: eagles belong to the order Falconiformes, including all true diurnal birds of prey or raptors, and within that order, to the suborder Accipitres, which comprise species variously known as hawks, eagles, buzzards, kites and vultures. Excluded from this suborder are the falcons (suborder Falcones) and New World vultures (suborder Cathartae). Within the Accipitres, the word eagle is generally applied to any large species which is not a vulture, i.e. a specialized carrion eater. Consequently, not all eagles are particularly closely related to each other. At least four different sets of birds feature in this book. These are, the Snake-eagles (including Short-toed and Bateleur); the Harpy and its relatives; eagles with legs feathered to the toes, including the Golden Eagle and others of the genus Aquila; and the sea eagles, which are considered fairly near relatives of the Old World vultures. The taxonomic order followed is basically that of Brown and Amadon (1968) but small alterations have been necessary to accommodate the layouts.

Eagles are traditionally regarded as regal birds. This is in part due to their size, and in part to their physical appearance. As we have seen, large size is implicit in the definition of an eagle, but it is instructive to examine their other kingly attributes, which tell us much about their way of life. The fierce yet noble appearance of the head is created largely by bill and eyes. The former, hooked as in all raptors, is also long and often very deep in eagles, indicating the large size of their prey, and the depth to which it may need to be plunged when consuming it. The eyes – often a striking golden color – are relatively huge and forwardly directed, reflecting their keen binocular vision. A bony shelf roofing over the eyes actually has a protective function, but creates a frowning appearance which provides the finishing touch. At rest, the imposing effect is enhanced by the long hunched "shoulders," strictly the forearm and wrist joints of the folded wings. These are a simple consequence of great wing length, and are most pronounced in the longest winged species. In the air, of course, the visual impact of the wings is overwhelming, due not only to their size, but to the upcurved, widely splayed flight feathers at the tips. These smooth out air flow and increase lift, and they are best developed in soarers such as the Black Eagle, which are also those with the greatest span. Forest eagles, such as the Harpy, have shorter but much broader wings, facilitating rapid movement between crowded trees. Perhaps the strangest flight outline is that of the Bateleur, with very long wings, often held swept back, and very short tail, features apparently designed for long sustained gliding at high speed.

The head and face may suggest power, but the feet reveal the real capacities of the bird, the length of talons particularly on the hind toe being closely related to the size of prey which the eagle is able to tackle. Slow motion filming has shown that in attack, a bird of prey flings its leg forward at the moment of impact, so that their speed is added to the flight speed of the bird. Such a blow is probably sufficient to kill many victims outright. Serpent eagles have proportionately very short toes, enabling their feet to completely surround the body of a snake to grip and crush more effectively. Despite their weaponry, however, many eagles evidently spend relatively little time actually hunting, and a good kill can provide enough food for several days. It is estimated for instance that an individual Golden Eagle requires less than 200lbs of food per year; spread over more than 5,000 acres of moorland, this hardly amounts to the wholesale rapacity alleged by its persecutors.

An eagle kill is, in fact, a rare event to witness, but fortunately many species make up for this with spectacular aerial courtship displays. These generally include a "sky-dance" – an alternating series of dives and ascents, either on an undulating forward course, a gradually descending "pot-hook" trajectory or a pendulum flight in which the bird repeatedly traverses the same arc of sky. Many other features of breeding biology are common to all eagles, including the reuse of nests, and the provision of fresh green sprays throughout the nesting cycle. One aspect which continues to puzzle and intrigue ornithologists is the "Cain and Abel" battle between sibling eaglets, in which the younger one often (in some species invariably) dies as a result of attacks by its nest mate. In such cases, it seems a waste of effort to lay two eggs at all; suggestions that the second egg acts as an insurance policy in case the first fails have yet to be backed up by watertight data. However, the habit may prove of unexpected value, for experiments in some species have shown that breeding success can be increased by rearing the younger eagle in captivity until shortly before fledging, when its reintroduction to the nest is accepted peaceably.

1　THE BALD EAGLE

HALIAEETUS LEUCOCEPHALUS

Though it is now accepted without question as the national emblem of the United States of America, the Bald Eagle at first faced opposition when nominated for this status. Benjamin Franklin maintained that the bird was a coward in the face of danger, and a mere scavenger in its feeding habits. Evidently, even by 1782, Bald Eagles in the mainland of the USA were showing the effects of too close association with man, for recent studies of more undisturbed populations in Alaska show that the Bald Eagle is a bold and efficient hunter, and often dauntingly aggressive in defense of its nest.

Alaska is, indeed, the last remaining area where Bald Eagles still survive in numbers, and can be studied under reasonably natural conditions. Elsewhere in the USA, the national bird has been drastically reduced in numbers. Though the decline appears to have been arrested it is nowhere numerous along the coast on which it once abounded. Direct persecution, loss of habitat due to development and environmental pollution all have played their part, and to see a large concentration of these splendid birds today, it is necessary to visit an Alaskan river during salmon spawning, or one of the remote islands in the Aleutian chain. On the rivers, particularly, numbers may be spectacular; counts along a 10 mile stretch of the Chilkat in mid-November have revealed totals of 3,000–4,000 eagles feeding on dead or spent male salmon.

One of the Bald Eagle's Aleutian outposts is Amchitka. Lying some 60 miles southwest of the Alaskan peninsula, this bleak little island, about 40 miles long and 3 miles wide sustained over 50 nesting pairs of eagles during the early 1970s, when they were the subject of an intensive study of breeding biology and ecology. Even here, though, the birds were not free from man's influence, but his effect was on balance beneficial: despite some breeding failures due to disturbance, the birds were enabled to maintain a high population by the presence of a garbage dump on the island. This dump was of particular value to immature birds, which generally showed more tendency to feed on carrion, doubtless because of their relative inexperience at hunting. The value of the dump became sadly evident after 1973, when the human settlement left and the dump was closed. A visit in 1974 showed that 1–3 year old birds were reduced in numbers by about 70 per cent; as no neighboring islands had experienced an influx of young eagles, this reduction almost certainly reflected increased mortality amongst young birds.

Adult Bald Eagles do take some carrion, of which common natural sources are stranded fish, whales and seals. In areas near civilization, road casualties provide another useful supply; opossums found in Florida nests were probably obtained in this way. However, Bald Eagles are also efficient and versatile hunters, able to exploit a wider range of potential food sources than almost any other raptor; on some Alaskan rivers, they have even been seen wading to seize fish, or hunting from the edge of ice floes. On Amchitka, the study team distinguished three principal hunting strategies: still-hunting from a perch, hunting from an aerial height, and hunting on direct flight. Perches selected for still-hunting were either cliffs and stalks overlooking the beach, or poles from which areas of tundra could be scanned. Prey obtained in this way included many fish of course, but also rats, sea otter pups, ptarmigan and waterfowl. Fish up to 12 inches in length are regularly taken, and can be devoured in less than a minute; the head is usually eaten first, and

Juvenile birds are uniformly brown; the adult plumage is assumed in stages over four to five years.

Adult

Young

Long broad wings, tail squarer than Steller's or White-tailed, white head and tail in adults only

when there are young to feed, the parents often consume the heads themselves, leaving the bodies for the young. Sea otter pups are vulnerable to eagle attack when their mothers dive for food, leaving them alone at the surface: the bleating cries they give at such times may unwittingly draw an eagle's attention to them. Pups are skinned and devoured methodically; the whole body is eaten, leaving the pelt inside-out with the cleaned leg bones still attached. Although sea otter pups may weigh nearly 4½lbs even larger prey is taken at times, although the distance it can be carried will be limited. Nevertheless, an Emperor Goose (about 6½lbs) was once seen to be captured on the beach and carried up to a rock stack on Amchitka.

Hunting from an aerial height appears to be directed principally to sea birds on the water, sometimes involving breathtaking stoops of over 300 feet. One nest on Amchitka contained the remains of 31 fulmars, probably caught in this way. When hunting in direct flight, eagles set out low over the ocean, dipping into the troughs of waves to conceal their approach, and in this way, auks are often surprised on the surface. Over the tundra, mounds and hummocks enable them to use similar tactics to catch ptarmigan. Bald Eagles are particularly deadly when they team up to hunt. Two or more eagles making successive stoops at ducks on a lake cause such panic and confusion to their prey that they are nearly always successful. Always opportunistic, Bald Eagles rarely miss the chance of an easy meal when a wounded bird is seen, and they are not above robbery, quite often harassing even Peregrine Falcons to make them drop their catch. Sea otters sometimes lose food as well as pups: their habit of floating on their backs while preparing prey with their front paws makes it an easy matter for an eagle to swoop across and snatch their prey from them. Despite these piratical tactics, it seems clear that a large proportion of the animals captured by the eagles were alive and healthy, and some birds are even taken in flight. The observers on Amchitka witnessed auks being snatched out of the air at nesting colonies, and on one occasion saw an eagle turn the tables on a group of gulls which were mobbing it, rolling over suddenly in flight to seize one of them in its talons. Water-birds, as might be expected, always predominate among those taken, and in Florida, the American coot heads the list of bird prey species.

Although the study on Amchitka gives a good picture of the Bald Eagle's feeding habits and ecology under fairly natural conditions, it is perhaps less typical where nesting and breeding biology are concerned. On treeless Aleutian islands, Bald Eagles are obliged to breed on rocky stacks (seeking always to select sites inaccessible to Arctic Foxes), and the nests they build in these bleak places are usually destroyed by wind and weather each winter. Throughout much of its range, however, the Bald Eagle is a tree nester and its eyries persist for years, added to each year to produce what must be the largest of all birds-nests, up to 11 feet deep, over 6 feet across, and weighing several hundred pounds. Sticks and branches with a lining of grass and other fine vegetation are the usual materials, but in treeless areas like Amchitka, the Bald Eagle may have to make do with kelp, driftwood and general rubbish to construct its nest. Where available green foliage may be added at any time in the breeding cycle, and sometimes the birds (old or young) are seen to eat a few leaves.

Bald Eagles at the nest. The national emblem of the USA, the survival of this magnificent bird is threatened by pollution.

Sea otter pups and spawning salmon are important prey of Northern birds. In the Southern USA, American coots are frequent victims.

Two eggs are the usual clutch, occasionally 3, and they are laid as early as possible in the winter, ranging from November in Florida to May in the far north. The incubation period apparently lasts 34-35 days – a shorter time than in its close relatives. Generally incubation is carried out by the female, but the male takes a small part in at least some cases. Interestingly, the female has the habit of covering the eggs with nest lining material when leaving the nest. Such behaviour is unknown in any other eagle, and Brown and Amadon expressed doubt about reports of it; however, the observers on Amchitka have confirmed that this does occur.

In most places, human intruders can visit a Bald Eagle's nest with impunity; the adults simply circle overhead, calling. This may be because in areas near humans, the more aggressive eagles have been shot, or it may be that in typical breeding habitats, the presence of trees near the nest discourages high speed aerial attacks. A quite different situation exists on Amchitka, where two of the researchers studying Bald Eagles have been struck by the birds with such force as to knock them to the ground and cause scalp lacerations. Even helicopters are readily attacked, one of the birds being so aggressive as to pursue any which ventured within a mile of the nest!

The young spend 10-11 weeks in the nest. Although "Cain and Abel" battles are rare in Bald Eagles, mortality is higher in nests with more than one young, apparently because of competition for food between the siblings. As in many birds of prey, the young may return to the nest to feed and rest for some time after fledging. Thereafter, they pass through a sequence of mottled plumages, finally reaching sexual maturity with white head and tail at about 5 years of age.

The fortunes of the Bald Eagle in its relations with man have fluctuated dramatically during its reign as America's national bird. For the first hundred years, all seemed well; the Bald Eagle remained generally popular, and one individual achieved great fame. This was "Old Abe", named after Abraham Lincoln, a captive eagle which was for some years the mascot of Company "C" of the 8th Wisconsin Regiment, and finally the Wisconsin State mascot, making frequent appearances at public events. Nevertheless, eagle numbers were even then declining due to habitat loss and shooting. This continued well into the twentieth century. Between 1915 and 1951, bounty was paid on a total of over 100,000 Bald Eagles shot in Alaska, supposedly to protect salmon stocks. Even when the species was granted special protection in 1940, Alaska was specifically excluded, and the bounty system there continued until 1953.

However, by this time, a more sinister threat had emerged, for the 1940s saw the start of large scale use of organo-chlorine insecticides such as DDT. All raptors are vulnerable to these, situated as they are at the end of a long food chain, but fish-eaters such as the Bald Eagle or Osprey are especially at risk because fish affected by toxic chemicals often rise to the surface, presenting easy opportunities for capture.

The effect of these chemicals is not necessarily to kill the eagle which takes them in; their action is usually more insidious, causing the birds to lay thin-shelled eggs which cannot hatch successfully. Thus, the only breeding pair of Bald Eagles in New York State had nested annually for 15 years, but fledged only a single offspring up to 1977. The cause of this was DDT which had been used for spraying nearby forests during the 1950s. Although this is now banned, it may be years yet before it totally disappears from the environment.

However, the future is not all bleak. Increasing public awareness of the Bald Eagle's plight has led to more effective measures to protect it, not only by strengthening the laws which forbid its direct persecution, but by controlling pollution and habitat erosion. Recently, the US Fish and Wildlife Service has appointed five regional Bald Eagle Recovery teams to co-ordinate plans for the bird's recovery. The species is now holding its own, with a population of some 1,200 breeding pairs in the lower 48 states. The numbers which can be seen there are swelled each winter by the arrival of up to 20,000 migrants from Canada and Alaska – and also, in the mid-USA from Florida, for, curiously, the birds which breed there move north outside the breeding season. Nevertheless, local concentrations in the colder months of the year must not lead to a false sense of complacency about the Bald Eagle's status. Years of dedicated work still lie ahead if its survival is to be assured.

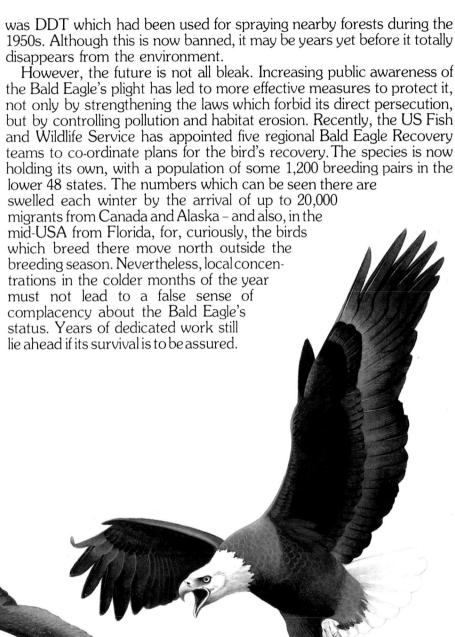

Bald eagles are not above piracy, and frequently harry Ospreys to rob them of fish.

Alaskan rivers attract hundreds of
Bald Eagles during November, when
salmon are spawning.

HALIAEETUS LEUCORYPHUS

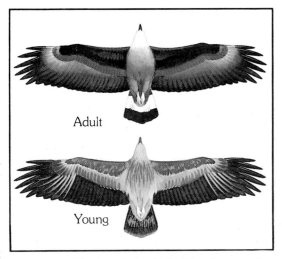

The banded tail of adults distinguishes them from other Eurasian Fish Eagles.

Slightly smaller than the White-tailed Eagle, Pallas's Fish Eagle is its inland counterpart, frequenting lakes, rivers and landlocked seas throughout central and southern Asia. Formerly a fairly regular visitor to the European parts of the USSR, and to Iraq, its range has contracted, and it is now only a rare visitor to these regions; its overall status is undocumented, but the trend is a distinctly downward one.

Adult Pallas's Fish Eagles are easily recognized by the black and white tail pattern and pale head merging into much darker body coloring. Immatures can cause problems, however, but can be distinguished from White-tailed Eagles by the rounded tail, and less heavy build, with quicker wingbeats. Similar in size to the Golden Eagle, they can at once be separated from it by the underwing pattern, with a pale band across the under coverts and a pale patch at the base of the primaries. Perching birds have a more horizontal attitude than their relatives. Not a very vocal bird, its usual call is a twice repeated bark. As eagles go, this is a relatively fearless species, often indifferent to man, especially if easy feeding can be obtained near his activities. Pallas's Fish Eagle takes not only fish, including many dead or stranded, but also young or disabled water birds up to goose size, and it has been known to kill pelicans and cranes. In general, its victims are unfit individuals and although this may seem to reflect poorly on the bird in anthropomorphic terms, it is fulfilling a valuable biological role by helping to weed out weaklings. It also harries other birds of prey to rob them of food.

Displays recorded are simply mutual soaring and calling, without any spectacular aerobatics. Nesting sites chosen are very variable; trees are used in the southern part of the range, but further north crags, or even sandbanks or reed beds may be utilized. Nests in trees grow with re-use from 4-6½ feet in diameter, while ground nests may be even larger.

Immatures resemble those of the White-tailed Sea Eagle but are smaller and the tail lacks a pale base.

Branches up to a yard long may be carried to the nest.

Opposite: Pallas's Fish Eagle is not a coastal species, preferring large inland waters.

Pallas's Fish Eagle spends much time on regular perches overlooking swamps and back waters.

Sticks and reeds form the bulk of the material, with a scanty lining of grass, green sprays and dung. Male and female are both involved in building, and during this period, either bird may bring food to the nest. They lay 2-4 eggs, clutches averaging larger in the south and incubation begins with the first egg. The female is entirely responsible for this duty, but the male brings food throughout. No reliable estimates of the incubation period are available, but at least 40 days seems likely. The young are looked after by the female at first, the male bringing food, but later both parents join in foraging. The fledging period appears to vary from 70 days to over 100, but is unlikely to be prolonged in the northern parts of the bird's range, where the summer is short, and both adults and immatures must be ready to move south in September or October.

3 AFRICAN FISH EAGLE

HALIAEETUS VOCIFER

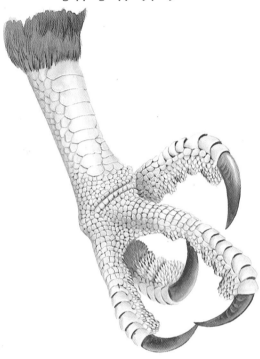

Like all fishing eagles the African Fish Eagle has roughened feet to aid in gripping slippery prey.

Opposite: From their perch on dead waterside trees African Fish Eagles repeatedly utter their loud ringing calls.

Ringing clear and high across the turquoise waters of a Rift Valley lake, the call of the Fish Eagle has been aptly called "the voice of Africa." The scientific name of this species is certainly appropriate, for few eagles are more vociferous than this one. A written version of its usual call is "weeah-hya-hya-hya", but neither letters nor sonograms can convey the thrilling and evocative sound that the bird utters daylong. Usually it is perched when calling, typically on a limb of a tall dead tree at the water's edge, but it may also call in flight. Whether perched or flying, it always throws its head up and back with each cry. Noisiest towards the beginning of the breeding season, the call is given by both sexes, but the female's voice is generally more high-pitched and thinner. A low "quok" is given by birds disturbed at the nest.

The African Fish Eagle is a bird of wooded water margins, whether river, lake or sea coast, occurring up to altitudes of 4,000 feet as a breeding bird, but usually in relatively low areas. It is mainly encountered in pairs in the breeding season or outside it, though in places where food is abundant many birds – up to 60 – may be seen together. Pairs usually roost together and share their kill; their general hunting strategy is to make flights out across the water, returning to the same perch if no prey has been caught. Where fish are plentiful, as on some of the East African lakes, about 650 acres of water is sufficient to supply the needs of a pair, but on small rivers, a 10-15 mile stretch may be required. Sometimes prey is sighted from the perch, but more usually while soaring. Fish may be captured by a swift plunge, or a slower, more controled approach. Large fish (about 4½ lbs is the usual maximum) are dragged along the surface towards the nearest rock or tree, and lifted ashore at the water's edge. The tale is often told about this species (as also about the osprey) that if it captures too large a fish, it will drown rather than let it go. Such stories can be disregarded, but at least one genuine case of a Fish Eagle in difficulties is recorded. An angler fishing by the Zambezi saw an eagle floating down river, and captured it by casting his line across it and reeling it in. He found that the bird had a leguaan (a large lizard) in its talons, and the reptile's tail was wrapped round the eagle's wing, preventing it from taking off, or even flapping to the bank.

Presumably this lizard had been swimming when captured, but Fish Eagles do not obtain all their food from the water. Stranded fish are consumed readily, and also carrion further inland. Peter Steyn witnessed one feeding with vultures on the carcass of a rhinoceros at the Hluhluwe Game Reserve in Zululand, and also mentions a pair which regularly brought "platannas" (clawed toads) to the nest. They sometimes take nestlings from heronries, and frequently capture waterbirds, including ducks and flamingos. There is a record of a Fish Eagle plucking a Malachite Kingfisher out of a bird ringer's mist net! Other fish eating species such as cormorants, pelicans, herons and ospreys are often harried to make them disgorge food, though attacks on the latter usually fail, and sometimes ospreys will pursue Fish Eagles. Overall, though, fish comprise 90 per cent of the diet with catfish and lungfish particularly frequent in East Africa, and mullets near the sea.

As with other African birds, breeding times vary widely over the continent, depending on local climatic conditions. In the northern tropics, laying begins about October, when the rains finish, and on the Equator during the dry season from June to August. In the southern

T. BOYER 81.

Adult

Young

The sharp contrast of white head and breast with dark underparts and dark under wings are field marks of the adult bird.

Immatures have boldly streaked underparts and the dingy tail terminates in a black band.

tropics, breeding commences about May to June, but further south still, dates are later, in South Africa during the southern spring. The general tendency to start breeding around the beginning of a dry season may be related to the fact that waters then become lower and clearer, which presumably facilitates hunting. As the breeding season draws near, pairs move into their territories, which may be quite small – Leslie Brown found 9 pairs on a 500 acre island in East Africa. They now become more vocal than ever, and aerial displays occur frequently. These involve soaring by either one bird or both together, and very occasionally talon grappling, during which the birds come cartwheeling down for several hundred yards.

Trees are preferred as nest sites, though cliffs may be used, and Peter Steyn shows a photograph of an unusual site on a finger of rock projecting out from the side of a gully. Chosen trees are usually large and difficult to climb – figs, tall acacias and Euphorbias are frequent and in South Africa, pines and eucalyptuses may be used. New nests may take 2-3 months to build, and are not always used the first season. Material added in subsequent years eventually enlarges them from some 60 × 12 inches to 70 × 50 inches. This pile of sticks has a lining of papyrus heads, grass and leaves, and weaver bird nests, which may be taken from colonies near the eagle's own nest. A pair may have up to 3 nests, but a single one is more usual; if there are 2 or 3, they are used in an entirely random sequence.

The 1-3 eggs are laid at 3 day intervals and incubation begins with the first. The female incubates, but the male may occasionally help, and each egg hatches in 44-45 days. Although the male often visits, he does not necessarily bring food; the female seems able to obtain enough food during short periods off the nest. The young hatch at 2 or 3 day intervals, but the extent of aggression between them seems to vary. Two often fledge from clutches of 3 eggs, but when 2 are laid, usually only 1 survives. In one nest studied 3 survived together for at least 2 weeks before 1 disappeared.

The young are brooded intensively by the female for 10 days, with the male bringing food. He continues to provide most of it for 40 days, after which the female shares this duty with him. Both birds spend much time together on the nest. At exposed nests, such as on top of Euphorbias, an important task for the female is to shelter the young from the sun. The young weigh about 2½ oz at three days old, 3 lbs at 24 days, when feathers first appear and 6 lbs at 50 days, when feathering is complete. From about 45-50 days, the young are able to feed themselves, and in the final week before fledging they move out onto branches and practice wing flapping. The first flight is made at 65-75 days; single eaglets may fledge more quickly than those in broods of 2. They remain near the nest for about 2 months, often returning to it to feed and roost during the first fortnight after fledging.

Leslie Brown studied a group of 7 pairs in East Africa over a 3 year period, during which time 1 pair reared young in each year, 1 pair did not breed at all, and the remainder fell at various points between these extremes. A total of 15 young were reared, giving a replacement rate of 0.54 young per pair, per year. A pair watched by Peter Steyn in South Africa over 6 years laid 15 eggs and reared 5 young – an average of 0.83 young per year. Breeding success may be reduced where nests are close together. Brown estimates their lifespan in the wild at 12-15 years. Though still widely distributed and common in many parts of Africa, it is threatened, like all fish eating raptors, by industrial chemicals.

An area particularly at risk is East Africa's Rift valley, with its chain of lakes; pollutants washed off the surrounding higher land tend to build up in the lakes, and environmentalists have been much concerned at the far reaching ecological consequences this could have. Similar problems are likely to occur elsewhere in the continent as developing countries become more industrialized unless safeguards are introduced now. Controls on the use of chemicals seems a small price to pay for the survival of some of Africa's finest wildlife attractions, not least this bird which has thrilled and captivated so many tourists.

The Rift Valley lakeside scenery is a typical setting for the African Fish Eagle.

4 WHITE-BELLIED SEA EAGLE

HALIAEETUS LEUCOGASTER

The coasts of south-east Asia attract increasing numbers of visitors, and few of them can have failed to notice the numerous fish-traps sited just off shore – structures of lashed poles from which nets can be anchored to catch fish moving with the tide. How many of them though notice the large gray and white birds so often perched like statues on these convenient vantage points? These graceful sentinels are White-bellied Sea Eagles, still, fortunately, a regular feature of the warm seas from India to Australia. Possibly many of the natives who construct the traps consider them as rivals, for they certainly include many fish in their diet. Equally, though, they prey upon sea snakes, feared by fishermen throughout the warm waters of the world. Like other snake eating birds of prey, their dexterity protects them from the potentially lethal strike of their victim.

When they are not seen perched on fish traps, rocks or trees, White-bellied Sea Eagles are usually encountered in flight, when the great size and the white body and wing coverts contrasting with black flight feathers immediately identify them; the browner immatures show a less marked contrast. Pairs are often seen together in flight, and regularly roost close to one another, often on a favorite tree which may be used regularly for a long time. Every morning and evening such pairs indulge in bouts of calling audible for long distances.

Hunting is carried out either by waiting patiently on their favorite perches, or by soaring: the range covered may be as small as a mile in diameter. Fish or sea snakes are captured by plunging from a height, but robbery of ospreys or other sea eagles are also regular food getting methods. White-bellied Sea Eagles will visit nesting colonies such as those of herons to take young birds; however, they are fairly easily intimidated, and well advanced young herons can successfully repel them. Small crocodiles and small mammals are taken, but carrion does not appear to attract the birds to any marked extent.

As the breeding season approaches, there is an increase of aerial activity, which appears to consist mainly of soaring accompanied by frequent calling, and mutual pursuit flights. The nest is usually situated high up in a tree, or occasionally a rock, and is built by both sexes; in a captive pair the male took the large share. It measures some 6 feet across and 3 feet deep, sometimes much more. Up to 3 nests may be found in a breeding territory, but it does not follow that they are used in rotation; the same one may be utilized many times in succession.

Two, sometimes 3 eggs are laid, white and coarsely textured. Incubation starts with the first, and appears to be mainly by the female; the incubation period has not been recorded. After hatching, the female again is the most involved parent, feeding and looking after the young while the male brings prey. As the young develop, the female spends more time away from the nest, and they gradually learn to feed for themselves. The young (usually 1, sometimes 2) fledge in about 65-70 days. Following this, they may be dependent on their parents for up to 6 further months.

An immature bird feeding on fish.

White-bellied Sea Eagles are frequently seen in pairs or small groups.

The contrast of black flight feathers and tail base with white body and wing linings distinguishes this eagle.

Sea snakes are a favourite prey of the White-bellied Sea Eagle.

The extensive mangroves fringing the coasts of Asia and Australia provide an ideal habitat for this species.

5 WHITE-TAILED SEA EAGLE

HALIAEETUS ALBICILLA

Averaging a third or more heavier than the Golden Eagle, and with longer, broader wings, this is Europe's largest eagle. Though less agile in flight than the Golden, and less rapacious in habits, its sheer size and almost vulture-like aerial silhouette render it a more visually impressive bird. Early in the nineteenth century it was a fairly numerous species around the coasts of Northern Scotland, with a stronghold on Skye, whose towering sea cliffs held several pairs. Sheep were its downfall. At a period when even humans were being ruthlessly evicted to give place to large scale sheep farming, it is scarcely to be wondered at that a large raptor suspected (however wrongly) of preying on lambs was systematically extirpated. Egg and skin collectors hastened the demise of the dwindling population, and by the end of the nineteenth century it had all but gone, though a pair lingered in Skye until 1916.

Bijleveld's analysis of the White-tailed Sea Eagle's status in Europe makes depressing reading, all the more so since the bird showed a trend towards recovery during and after the Second World War. This has been more than canceled out since by continued persecution, habitat destruction and the insidious effects of persistent organo-chlorine insecticides. Norway remains the stronghold of the species, but it is sad to record its decline in other parts of Scandinavia. In Iceland, the Sea Eagle was generally distributed during the last century, but it is now confined to the west coast. Possibly 150 pairs were to be found in the country early in the 1800s, but by 1890, 41 pairs were known, 11 in 1910 and 7 in 1921. This steep decline is traceable mainly to the poisons regularly put out for Arctic Foxes and Ravens; ironically, both species survive in much larger numbers than the White-tailed Sea Eagle. The practice of poisoning fortunately dwindled as the twentieth century advanced, and by 1929, 14 pairs were counted, mainly in the West. Censuses carried out since the war indicate a population of about 40 pairs, which seems to be stable, though the future depends on the effectiveness of the laws against poisoning enacted by Parliament in 1964 and 1966.

In Sweden, the decrease seems to have been equally dramatic. Accounts during the mid-nineteenth century indicate that the bird was generally common in all suitable habitats, but by the early years of the twentieth it appeared to be on the verge of extinction. During the 1920s, the remaining population was in the region of 20 pairs, but the respite afforded by the war years allowed this number to double. Since the 1960s, the number of breeding pairs appears to have been about 40, declining slowly, but a sinister pointer for the future emerged from the breeding results. During the late 1960s and early '70s, the number of young produced declined gradually to 4 in 1973. This reduction coincided with the appearance of alarming quantities of DDT, and related compounds, and of polychlorbiphenyls in birds, eggs and nestlings. At present, the situation shows some remission, presumably due to a reduction in use of persistent insecticides. In Finland, another one-time stronghold, the situation is still worse. By the mid '60s, the population had dwindled to no more than 20 pairs, and very few young have been produced since this time. Even Denmark harboured some 50 pairs in 1880, but by 1912 the species had ceased to breed there, although an isolated case of successful breeding occurred in 1954, since when it has disappeared again. Greenland, of course, is administered by

Immatures have a dark tail with the base mottled white.

The long, very broad wings and white wedge-shaped tail are diagnostic of the adult in flight.

Opposite: The White-tailed Sea Eagle is currently subject of a re-introduction trial in Scotland.

Denmark, and here a population of 50-80 pairs survives in the West. Though protected by law, persecution still takes place. This population ranks as a distinct subspecies, averaging larger than other White-tailed Sea Eagles.

The White-tailed Sea Eagle's survival in Norway must owe much to the sheer extent of its mountainous coastline, and the rather low and scattered human population. Even here, though, extensive reduction has taken place, and it has disappeared from many former haunts, particularly in the South. Willgohs, who has studied its distribution in Norway in great detail, estimates that in 414 breeding territories known since 1850, 221 were still occupied in the period between 1956 and 1960, 70 were definitely deserted, and 123 were probably occupied. 85 per cent of the total population is concentrated between the northern part of Sor-Trondelag and Tanafjord in East Finmark. A total Norwegian population of about 350 pairs in the 1960s was estimated by Willgohs. Although a more recent study suggests this is too high, it seems that the situation is at present stable.

In Continental Europe, the main stronghold of the species lies in Pomerania and Mecklenburg, in what is now East Germany. Up to the beginning of the nineteenth century, it appears to have been numerous in these areas, with 47 breeding places known in Mecklenburg alone. By the beginning of the twentieth century, however, its number had dwindled to a mere 2 or 3 pairs, as a result of direct persecution. After the First World War, protection was introduced, and the species gradually increased up to the late 1950s, during which time it recolonized in parts of West Germany, from which it had disappeared in 1920. However, there has been a decline since that time, coinciding with heavy use of chemical pesticides. In East Germany as a whole, a possible population of 110-120 pairs may still exist, but breeding results are poor, and the situation still gives grave cause for concern. Poland supported a large and widely distributed population during the last century, but this had been reduced to only a few pairs by the beginning of the twentieth. There has been some recovery recently, and a total of 40-50 pairs was estimated in 1970. A similar history can be given for Rumania and northern Greece, though with no evidence of recovery. From Yugoslavia, Hungary and Bulgaria, where the species once abounded, it has now all but disappeared.

European Russia has followed the same general pattern of catastrophic reduction during the nineteenth century, followed by a period of recovery and then renewed decline since the introduction of chemical pesticides. The remainder of the USSR, however, still holds a large population, though there is little information on its fortunes. Even in these remote regions, persecution and decline seems likely. During 1963, on an expedition to the Caspian Sea, I saw White-tailed Eagles fairly common near the Eastern border of Iran with the USSR, and probably good numbers still exist in this region. In Central Asia and Siberia the bird breeds in mountainous regions, at altitudes up to 6,500 feet, and in such places, inaccessibility may allow the bird to survive.

The White-tailed Sea Eagle may yet make conservation history, however. One attempt has already been made to re-introduce it to Scotland, using four young birds taken from Norway, where a sizeable population still exists. This attempt, on Fair Isle, was a failure, 3 of the

Guillemots, gull chicks and Eider ducks are part of this eagle's varied diet.

eagles wandering off and disappearing, while one probably died there. Nevertheless, the lessons learned may yet be applied to further attempts. Clearly the number introduced needs to be greater, and a larger island is required to establish them: mainland sites must be rejected because of their vulnerability. A renewed attempt is now in progress on the island of Rhum, a National Nature Reserve. Leslie Brown has proposed a scheme involving fostering Sea Eagles' eggs out to Golden Eagles over a period of 5-10 years; unorthodox and controversial as this may sound, it could yet prove to be the most effective method of re-establishing this splendid bird of prey in Britain.

Although British and Norwegian populations have in general fully merited the name of sea eagle, the inland populations in Germany, Sweden and elsewhere forage by lakes and rivers, using trees as nest sites. Nevertheless, the bird is firmly associated in most people's minds with wild, rocky coasts. Accordingly, its diet includes a large proportion of such items as sea birds, seal pups and fish, but it has to be said that a good deal of this is taken as carrion; though capable of tackling prey up to the size of a roe deer calf, the White-tailed Sea Eagle kills a much smaller proportion of its prey than does the Golden. Hunting flights are generally low over the water, relying a good deal on surprise, and diving seabirds such as cormorants, eiders or auks are particularly vulnerable to sea eagle attacks, because their repeated attempts to escape by diving eventually exhaust them; the Eagle is thus assured of success by mere persistence. Gulls are also taken, particularly kittiwakes, but fulmars are another matter; the oily fluid which they squirt from their mouths in self defence can have disastrous effects on the plumage which it hits, causing severe impairment of flying ability and insulation. The introduced young bird which is believed to have died on Fair Isle evidently met its end in this way, for it was seen a few days before its disappearance in a sorry condition, its feathers matted with oil resembling that ejected by fulmars. Such an incident is doubtless the result of inexperience; in general, sea eagles appear to leave fulmars strictly alone. Obviously fish figure prominently in the eagle's diet, and some of these are actually captured, when swimming near the surface. However, beach washed fish are also readily eaten, and where they occur, ospreys are often harried to rob them of their catches.

The breeding cycle commences with aerial "displays" which are on the whole less dashing than in many eagles, reflecting the bird's generally rather ponderous and heavy flight. Most spectacular to witness are the aerobatics which ensue when the male dives at the female: rolling over, she locks talons with him, following which the pair go spinning downwards in cartwheel fashion, to separate just above the sea or ground. A pair of sea eagles will have several nests in its breeding area, and unless a new one is started, early spring activity consists of the refurbishing of one of these with branches, sticks and a fresh lining of grasses and similar material. Mating usually takes place near the nest.

The clutch size average a little over 2 in Norwegian and Icelandic populations studied, rather more than in the Golden Eagle. Both parents incubate, with the male taking a quarter or a third share of this duty by day, though his mate alone broods at night. Estimates of incubation period vary from 38-45 days. Since this begins with the first egg, the young hatch at different times, as in most eagles. However, they appear much more inclined to settle down peaceably together than is the case in most species, so that the number reared averages more than in most other eagles. This could prove an asset in any re-introduction scheme based on fostering out eggs; the rearing of large broods might be further facilitated by supplementary feeding.

During the early part of the fledging period, most food is supplied by the male, but after 5 or 6 weeks, the female joins him in hunting. The young make their first flights after some 10-13 weeks but remain around the nest, dependent on their parents, for a further two months. At this age, they have dark brown tails, and completely white ones are not attained until 3 or 4 years of age. Mortality is high in the first autumn, and Brown estimates that probably barely a quarter of young sea eagles survive to the age of first breeding, at 4-5 years. Allowing for this mortality, and the overall low rate of reproduction, it is clear that once adulthood is attained, the lifespan must be considerable in order to maintain the population. White-tailed Eagles have lived for 45 years in captivity, though few could be expected to attain such an age in the wild.

Remote sea cliffs and fjords are a typical habitat in Northern Europe.

6 STELLER'S SEA EAGLE

HALIAEETUS PELAGICUS

Adult

Young

In flight the white tail appears even more wedge shaped than that of the White-tailed Sea Eagle.

Prey up to the size of geese are part of this eagle's diet.

On average, this may be the world's largest eagle, some females weighing nearly 30 lbs though 13-15 is probably more usual. It is certainly one of the most impressive: though the feet and talons are of modest proportions as in other sea eagles, the striking plumage pattern, massive orange bill and sheer size lend it a truly regal appearance. Its habits – though less well known than those of its relatives – seem to be well in keeping with this impression, for its prey include a range of large and active species. Among these are birds up to the size of Capercaillies and geese, while young seals, sable and Arctic Fox are numbered with the mammalian prey. However, as in the Bald Eagle, stranded salmon are a major food source when available, and its principal wintering areas are around the rivers where these come to spawn. Crabs, molluscs and some carrion are also taken, the latter mainly by immature birds, which sometimes visit slaughterhouses to find offal. Comparatively little time is actually spent in flight, though it may well be that, as in the Bald Eagle, the bird takes much of its prey by "still hunting". Favorite perches include trees, rocks, walls and gravel banks in rivers.

The usual call is a deep, barking cry, but a gull-like note is used during display. As far as recorded, this consists simply of soaring above the nesting site, though very probably more complicated and spectacular aerobatics occur as in other sea eagles. The huge nests are generally built in trees and used year after year. They may be up to 11 feet wide and sited up to 100 feet in height. Two eggs (sometimes 1 or 3) are laid in late April or early May. Like those of the White-tailed and Bald Eagles

Adults have a white leading edge to the wing. Size and coloration render this one of the world's most impressive eagles.

The bill is exceptionally deep and strongly arched.

they are unmarked whitish. Young hatch in early June after an incubation period estimated at 38-45 days. One young only is usually reared, but sometimes as many as 3 may be fledged. The young leave the nest in August, having spent about 10 weeks there.

The limited geographical range of Steller's Eagle makes it potentially vulnerable, and doubtless it is subject to some of the same pressures as its relatives where it comes into contact with humanity. Some of the breeding places on the remote parts of Kamschatka, Sakhalin and North Korea may be relatively safe, but during winter these birds move South to find unfrozen areas of water, ranging as far as Japan and South Korea. In such areas it is at greater risk from both pollution and direct persecution. However, the resident race of South Korea is still tolerably common, and more frequently seen than the northern form. It is distinguished by slightly smaller size, and an all-black plumage, save for the white tail. In all plumages, Steller's Sea Eagles can be identified by the deep bill and strongly wedge-shaped tail – useful features where its range overlaps that of the White-tailed Eagle, or in the case of stragglers to Alaskan islands where confusion with the Bald Eagle might occur.

Immatures are best distinguished from those of the White-tailed Sea Eagle by bill shape.

The Korean form has all black head and shoulders.

Bleak sea coasts and rivers are the
home of Steller's Sea Eagle.

7 SHORT-TOED EAGLE

CIRCAETUS GALLICUS

Opposite: Europe's only Serpent Eagle feeds almost exclusively on snakes.

Telegraph poles provide useful perches for birds of prey.

Europe's only Snake-Eagle, one might have hoped that the Short-toed Eagle would enjoy encouragement rather than persecution, given the general antipathy of humans towards serpents. Ignorance prevails, however, and this unusual and interesting bird of prey is persecuted along with the rest, and has largely disappeared from Central Europe as a result. Moreover, modern agricultural practices have drastically reduced the reptile populations on which it depends in many areas. Spain is now its headquarters in Europe, with an estimated 3,000 pairs in 1977, followed by France, with about 400 pairs, and Poland, with 50-100 pairs. Elsewhere, only a handful survive.

Recognition of the Short-toed Eagle should present relatively few problems. Usually seen overhead, it is the only large European raptor with almost entirely whitish underparts contrasting with a dark head and upper breast. Moreover, when hunting, it frequently hovers; buzzards occasionally do so, but, are generally darker and more heavily marked below. As an alternative to hovering, it may still hunt from a perch, or even descend to the ground and forage on foot. Whatever method is adopted, however, snakes are the principal object of its search. A wide variety of them have been recorded in its diet, both venomous and non-venomous, but there seems to be a definite bias towards non-venomous species, even in areas where venomous ones (e.g. adders) are plentiful. The Short-toed Eagle is certainly not immune from snake venom, though its heavily scaled legs and thick down may protect it from bites to some extent; however its main safeguard is its own speed and dexterity in capturing and killing them. When a snake is located, the eagle swoops, then checks its descent at the last moment before seizing its victim. This is normally carried up into the air, where the talons are used to crush the head and neck, or tear the head off. It can then be taken to a perch to be eaten at leisure. Large snakes are sometimes attacked and killed on the ground, and torn up before being carried off. Most are swallowed head first, in a series of gulps. Snakes up to 3 feet long are recorded as prey in Europe, and occasional ones nearly twice this length in India.

The small proportion of its diet which does not consist of snakes is mainly composed of lizards, but a few other items may vary it. Birds ranging from finches up to guinea fowl in size are recorded, but most are either nestlings, or injured individuals. A few mammals are taken, such as voles, rats, and moles up to rabbits and hares. Occasional invertebrates are taken, such as worms, beetles and slugs. It is estimated that the daily requirements of an adult are equivalent to 1 or 2 medium sized snakes; nestlings need rather more to sustain their rate of growth, estimated at about 4-4½ oz or 2-3 snakes per day.

The Short-toed Eagle is monogamous, but in the migratory populations of Europe, pairs break up at the end of the breeding season, though the same individuals may well pair again in the next. Aerial displays include a version of the undulating "sky-dance" seen in other eagles. Although this follows a relatively gentle flat trajectory by comparison with many other species, it is of interest for the fact that the bird often carries a snake (sometimes a lizard or a twig) in the bill, and varies the display by dropping this and catching it again. The Short-toed Eagle is a highly vocal bird, and often calls during its displays. Its vocalizations generally have a fluty, musical quality, sometimes

In open country the Short-toed Eagle frequently hovers whilst searching for prey.

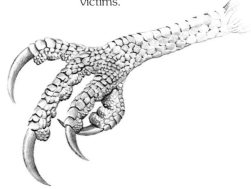

The short toes are ideally suited to grasping the slippery bodies of victims.

reminiscent of a Golden Oriole. Strongly territorial, they react to intruders in their territory with a characteristic flight-threat posture, with neck extended, wings spread and held slightly forward and legs dangled. In this attitude, and calling all the time, it approaches the other bird only to revert to normal flight as a chase develops in which they circle around each other while gaining height. Curiously, despite such aggressiveness, intrusions near the nest by other individuals are rather common in this species, and at one eyrie it was shown that 3 different adults brought snakes to the chick. "Helpers" at the nest are known in a number of other groups of birds, but for such behaviour to occur in the face of outright hostility by the parents is strange indeed. Other members of its own species are not the only intruders to arouse hostility: even humans may sometimes be vigorously mobbed, but occasionally a distraction display may be performed, in which the bird drops off the nest and shuffles away as though injured.

Nest building is carried out by both sexes, the male generally bringing material in his bill, the female actually constructing it. Old nests are sometimes reused, but not with the regularity of many larger eagles. The nest is rather a small one for a raptor of this size; it measures 1½ to 3 feet across, and about 12 inches deep. It is composed of sticks, and has a deep cup lined with green leaves and sprays of pine. A replacement nest

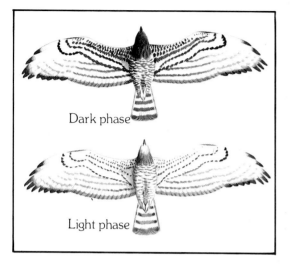

Dark phase

Light phase

Adults seen overhead appear generally white with 2 or 3 dark bars crossing flight feathers and tail.

Lightly wooded open country is this eagle's preferred habitat.

can be made in as little as 4 days, though 2-3 weeks is usual with the initial one.

Only a single egg is laid, but may be replaced if lost. Incubation is carried out mainly by the female, and lasts 45-47 days. The young one is brooded continuously while small, and fed by the female, though it is the male who brings the food. As it grows older, it can eventually pull a snake from the crop of its parent. The chick has a distinctive clucking food call, and a more disyllabic version when begging to be brooded. It adopts a defensive posture if disturbed from about 8 weeks old, and occasionally attacks a human intruder, striking at the eyes. Feathers begin to appear at 4 weeks old, and the cover is complete by 7 weeks. The fledging period is about 70-75 days, but the young bird may move out onto surrounding branches as early as 60 days. The period of subsequent independence from the parents is not known.

European populations of Short-toed Eagles are all migratory, western birds wintering in northern tropical Africa, while those from the east, winter in Indian sub-continent. Prior to migration from Europe, there is a period of dispersal from the breeding areas, beginning in early August. The main period of departure from Europe starts in mid September and continues until mid October. Although some apparently cross wide areas of the Mediterranean, the majority reach winter quarters via Gibraltar, the Sicilian Channel, the Bosphorous and the Caucasus. Largest numbers are seen at Gibraltar, where 9,040 were counted during the autumn of 1972, with peaks of 834 on 30th September, and 1,328 on 1st October. The spring return is more evenly spread and less spectacular; most arrive back in their breeding areas from mid March to mid April.

8 BATELEUR

TERATHOPIUS ECAUDATUS

Opposite: The exceptionally long wings are an adaptation of high speed gliding flight.

Immatures bear an interesting resemblance to the closely related Serpent Eagles.

Soaring over bushveldt or grasslands, the distinctive flight silhouette of the Bateleur is as characteristically African as giraffes or acacia trees. The eighteenth century French naturalist Le Vaillant gave it its name, which can mean tumbler, juggler or tightrope-walker, doubtless an allusion to either the aerobatics of which it is capable, or the rocking motion of its flight as it glides across country. Seen overhead, its outline is unlike any other eagle's, with exceptionally long wings, narrowing sharply at the tips, and an extremely short tail. The whole effect is rendered more striking by the contrast between white under wing coverts and the black tipped flight feathers and black body. It is easy to distinguish the sexes in flight; from below the female shows a much narrower black border to the trailing edge of the wing than the male, while the upperside of her wing bears a large whitish patch which her mate lacks.

Features of structure and plumage, especially in immature birds, give strong evidence that the Bateleur is closely related to the Snake Eagles, but many features of its behavior and temperament differ sharply from those of other raptors. One such characteristic is its extreme wariness when humans are near the nest. Although aggressive enough to stoop at intruders, it will not return to eggs or young until they have moved well clear of the nest; thus attempts to photograph birds at the nest, even from a hide, would cause desertion. A remarkable piece of behaviour witnessed by Peter Steyn when visiting a nest consisted of perching near it, flapping the wings limply and uttering a chattering call, while at the same time permitting an unusually close approach. He suggests that this may be a distraction display, akin to the "injury-feigning" of many other birds. If so, this is a piece of behaviour unique among raptors. An equally unusual aspect of its breeding biology is the frequent presence of a third bird near the nest. Usually this is a juvenile or immature, but quite commonly an adult, which may even roost with the male of the pair while the female is incubating.

Bateleur Eagles build nests of sticks, lined with sprays of green material, from about 20-65 feet up in a tree. Rather small at first, they are re-used in later years, and added to, so that they eventually become quite substantial structures. Occasionally the old nests of other birds of prey are taken over and refurbished. The "Cain and Abel" situation does not arise in the Bateleur, for only 1 egg is laid and 1 eaglet reared. Incubation is usually entirely by the female, and lasts about 6 weeks. Records indicate that breeding can take place at almost any time of the year, regardless of local conditions. The chick which hatches is surprisingly deeply colored, with buff down on head, neck and underparts, contrasting with dark brown on back and wings. At first it appears weaker than most eaglets, with a strongly wrinkled cere. Feathers start to appear from about 3 weeks, but it will be some 3- months before the young bird makes its first flight. Even after this it may return to the nest for a time. Bateleurs do not breed every year, and the young do not acquire fully adult plumage – a rough indicator of sexual maturity – until 6 years old. It follows that the life span must be considerable, even in the wild.

Among Zulus and related peoples of South Africa, the Bateleur is known as the "Warrior bird", and has a reputation strongly connected with battles and death. Another of its names among these people means

Snakes, ground squirrels and
francolins are regular prey.

The Bateleur inhabits the great
savannahs and grasslands of Africa.

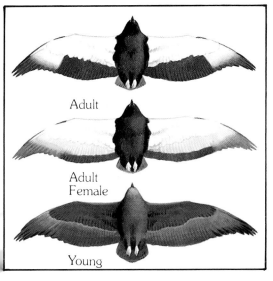

Adult

Adult
Female

Young

In flight males show a broader dark band on trailing edge of wing.

"eater of the warriors," and this could have a macabre basis of fact, for much of the Bateleur's food consists of carrion – another way in which it differs from its Snake Eagle relatives. Nevertheless, it does also take some reptiles, including even such deadly species as the Puff Adder. Extensive studies of the Bateleur have also revealed the remains of many birds in its nests, which suggests that it may take some of these in flight. Certainly it is not averse to piracy, launching aerial attacks on other raptors and carrion feeders, apparently with the intention of making them drop or disgorge prey.

Bateleurs in captivity become amazingly tame. Unlike many other pet birds, which appear at best to endure their owner's caresses. Bateleurs seem clearly to enjoy being stroked and lower their heads to solicit this. In the wild, however, there is some evidence of reduction in numbers. Obviously, this highly sensitive species would be vulnerable to any increase in human disturbance, and in the long term, its survival may become increasingly dependent on setting aside large tracts of land for purely conservational use.

At rest females can be distinguished by the broad pale band across the secondaries.

9 CRESTED SERPENT EAGLE

SPILORNIS CHEELA

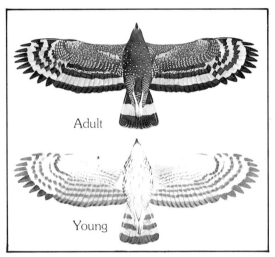

Adult

Young

In flight the wings and tail always show a strongly barred pattern, although color of underpart varies greatly among the various races.

Opposite: The Crested Serpent Eagle shows great geographic variation: the race depicted here is that from Northern India.

Below: an immature bird.

Still widely distributed in Asia, the Crested Serpent Eagle is nonetheless dependent on forest cover – a habitat which is steadily being eroded throughout the world, and especially in the tropics. This is a variable species, with 21 geographical races currently recognized; those from temperate areas tend to be paler than those from the tropics; both in adult and immature plumages. Although continuous forest is its preferred habitat, it may hunt in open grasslands or even villages and cultivated areas, but the home range of a pair will always contain at least some woodland.

Hunting is carried out mainly by watching from a perch, usually a well concealed one; when a victim is seen, the bird simply drops onto it. Some prey may, however, be located while flying, as Whitehead, the Bornean naturalist, noticed that a Crested Serpent Eagle regularly beat along a dried up river bed, where lizards and snakes could often be seen out in the open. Its prey includes many tree snakes, and occasional small mammals. It has been reported as taking ducks and game birds in India, but this seems to be exceptional. In Borneo, frogs, millipedes, scorpions and locusts have also been recorded as prey.

This is a noisy species, often crying on the wing, and audible from a great height. The usual call is a whistling scream, consisting of several short notes, rising in pitch, followed by 3-4 longer squeals. Calling is most frequent and pronounced in the soaring display flights performed during the breeding season. More spectacular aerobatics including dives and rolls, are also sometimes performed. Like other snake eagles, the Crested Serpent Eagle builds a relatively small nest, usually a fresh one each year. It is commonly sited halfway up a tree from 10-75 feet up, often overlooking a forest stream or swampy area. The twigs used for the nest are usually broken off from live branches, and green leaves from the lining of the deep central cup. Both male and female build. One egg is the usual clutch, and hatches in 35-37 days. Both parents feed the young bird, which fledges at about 60 days.

Dense forest cover is the preferred habitat of this eagle.

10 CELEBES SERPENT EAGLE

SPILORNIS RUFIPECTUS

Closely related to the widely distributed Crested Serpent Eagle of Asia, this distinct species is confined to Sulawesi (Celebes and Sula Islands). At present it is still reasonably common, but it is to be hoped that Sulawesi will not suffer an expansion of human population similar to that of Java, for it is doubtful whether it could survive such pressure. The destruction of forests which is occurring on the island may affect it less than some birds of prey, for it prefers open savannah or even cultivated areas for hunting, but some intermixture with wooded strips and copses is needed; large areas of unbroken rice paddy are unlikely to suit it.

Small snakes, lizards and occasional rodents form its diet, and like the Crested Serpent Eagle it hunts from perches, often sitting patiently for hours at a time waiting for prey to show itself. It is frequently seen in company with the Woolly-necked Stork, also a snake eater, probably because both are attracted to the same hunting areas. The Celebes Serpent Eagle is often seen on the wing, however, and frequently utters a clear whistling scream. Such soaring flights have a display function, but surprisingly, there is no information on the nests, eggs or breeding biology of this bird. Probably, like the Crested Serpent Eagle, it builds a relatively small stick nest in a tree and lays a single egg, incubated entirely by the female.

The rufous breast distinguishes this species from the Crested Serpent Eagle. This eagle occurs in more open areas than the Crested Serpent Eagle, quite often near cultivation.

EUTRIORCHIS ASTUR

This is probably the smallest species included in this book, and would scarcely qualify for the name of eagle were it not that it is clearly related to other Serpent Eagles, with the same characteristically shaped crest and crown feathers as in those of the genus Spilornis. Its nearest relative, however, may be the Congo Serpent Eagle, which it resembles in its unusually long tail. Certainly this is one of the most mysterious of the world's eagles, and possibly the rarest. It is known to inhabit humid forest in the north-east of Madagascar, up to moderate heights, and has been seen perching on large trees, or making short flights between them. Probably it hunts from perches as do other forest dwelling Serpent Eagles, though the rather Goshawk-like shape might indicate that more active methods are also employed. The only food item recorded is a chameleon - a group of lizards which abound in Madagascar. Whether it specializes on these creatures like the Cuckoo Roller, another native of the island, or whether it takes a broader range of prey will have to await further study. So, too, will its breeding habits, for at present no nest has ever been discovered. Let us hope it survives to make this possible.

The Madagascar Serpent Eagle is one of the world's rarest and least known eagles. Humid forest is the usual habitat for this species.

12 GUYANA CRESTED EAGLE

MORPHNUS GUIANENSIS

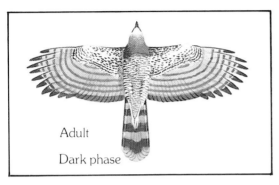

Adult

Dark phase

Dark phase bird in flight. The short, broad wings and long tail are characteristics in all plumages.

This handsome but little known eagle is clearly a close relative of the Harpy Eagle, but smaller and more lightly built. It is longer tailed than the Harpy, with a single crest, not a divided one. The long tail and short broad wings produce a rather Goshawk like silhouette in flight. Adults occur in two color phases, with some intermediate types. The pale phase has most of the underparts whitish, while in the dark phase they are heavily barred with black.

It is said to prefer the warmest and most humid regions of the heavy jungle it inhabits, and particularly the edges of rivers. Though sometimes seen in soaring flight, it also spends much of its time perched motionless high up in tall trees. Monkeys, opossums, birds and reptiles are recorded as prey. There is equally little information on its breeding habits. It is said to build a huge nest in the highest forest trees. A single egg, said to be of this species, is cream coloured, with pale markings.

Opposite: An adult Guyana Crested Eagle of the pale colour form.

The dense humid tropical forests are the habitat of this eagle.

An immature bird.

13 HARPY EAGLE

HARPIA HARPYJA

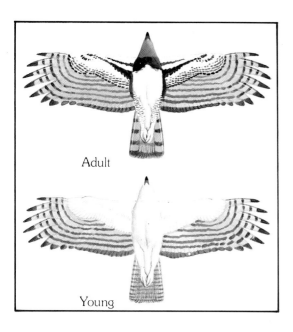

Adult

Young

Adult has broad short wings, black
breast band and strongly barred tail.

Undoubtedly the world's most powerful eagle, the Harpy is not the largest in terms of weight, and its wing span is quite moderate. What does set it apart from others is the immense size of the talons, and the girth of the tarsi which carry them. At first sight, the development of the feet seems almost excessive: though the Harpy Eagle takes sizeable animals such as sloths and howler monkeys, its victims average no larger than those of several other eagles. When the eagle is seen in action, however, their value becomes clearer. Most of its prey are arboreal, and at the moment of capture are usually clinging tightly to branches; in the case of sloths, this grip may be extremely strong. The eagle's technique is to snatch them from the trees, almost without a break in its flight – there is an excellent piece of slow motion film made in Guyana showing a Harpy Eagle taking a sloth hanging under a branch, rolling adroitly to pass under the bough, seizing the hapless creature, and continuing on in a single swift manoeuvre. To perform this operation effectively requires not only the high momentum resulting from the bird's weight and speed, but also a secure first-time grip. It seems possible, also, that the risks of injury to the bird are high in this type of attack, so that the great thickness of the tarsi may be in part a safety factor.

Seen in its natural habitat of South or Central American rain forest, the Harpy Eagle's large size seems less striking, and it can be surprisingly inconspicuous. Though occasionally seen soaring, aerial displays do not appear highly developed in this species, and it is more likely to be encountered dashing between the limbs of huge trees in pursuit of prey. In such situations, the value of its relatively short wings is easily seen. Adults occasionally give loud wailing calls, but it is the high-pitched hunger screams of young birds that are most likely to draw attention to it.

Most of our knowledge of the Harpy Eagle's breeding biology relates to two regularly used nesting places in the Kanuka Mountains of Southern Guyana studied by Fowler and Cope. Nests are built at a great height, usually in forest giants emerging above the main canopy: silk-cotton trees are favored in Guyana.   They are sited in major forks, preferably with nearby horizontal limbs on which the birds can perch. Sticks up to 1½ inches in diameter form the bulk of the nest, which can be up to 5 feet across and 3 feet deep. The bowl of the nest is lined with green leaves, or in one case, sloth hair. It seems that 2 eggs are laid at least sometimes, but the incubation period is unknown. The pairs studied by Fowler and Cope were far past this stage, having young capable of flight, but still dependent on their parents. Though not confined to the nest tree, they remained in its vicinity, uttering hunger screams. The intervals between feeding them were very long, as much as 10 days in one case. Their hunger screams increased in frequency and intensity through their period of fasting, eventually becoming more of a whine, each call being accompanied by a wing flap made with a forward motion at the wrist. This flashed the white under wing coverts conspicuously, probably adding to the effect of the calls in stimulating the adults to bring food. The young eagles roosted on the top branches of the silk cottons on most nights, especially if they had not eaten. Large limbs are preferred as perches, possibly because the smaller ones are studded with cone shaped spikes. Calling began about half an hour after

Previous page: Endowed with
exceptionally heavy legs and talons
this is undoubtedly the world's most
powerful eagle.

Pale head and underparts distinguish
the immature.

sunrise, and was most intense in early morning and mid-afternoon.

When an adult eventually appeared with food, the juveniles became excited and started to call more frequently well before it reached them. Their response to her arrival was to chase her away almost as soon as she had dropped it, and then mantle over it screaming until the adult left the area. One adult's response to this treatment was to launch a furious attack on the leaves and branches of a neighboring tree. It is tempting to see this as indicating frustration at its treatment, though the true cause may have been connected with the presence of human observers or their climbing ropes. One juvenile made mock "killing" attacks on a dead coatimundi which had just been delivered. Such behaviour is doubtless a preparation for eventual independent hunting, but at the stage they were observed – 8-10 months old – the young were still showing no inclination to kill for themselves. When live prey were tethered on the ground below, they flew part way down to look at it, but proceeded no further. However, dead prey placed in a tree attracted them quickly. The young fed unhurriedly, even after a long fast, first detaching fur carefully with a sideways action of the beak. A dead monkey tied in a tree as bait was detached and carried around for several hours before beginning to eat it. With such a long period of dependence, it is evident that the Harpy Eagle can breed at most only once every 2 years – an arrangement typical of very large eagles.

Towards the end of their observations Fowler and Cope captured an adult female and a juvenile of each sex for further study, using baited snares to trap them. Strangely, the adult seemed docile almost from the beginning, and ate readily from the fist on her second day. After 2 weeks, she could be flown free in her home area and be recalled for a feed of meat. While flying her, it was possible to observe her hunting techniques closely. She flew powerfully and very fast through the forest in pursuit of prey, manoeuvring with great skill between the trees, and sometimes climbing almost vertically. While seeking prey, she moved short distances from perch to perch, listening and watching for extended periods at each one. The juvenile eagles were less easy to train, and more excitable and unpredictable in their reactions. It was found that the captive birds needed on average 7½ oz of meat per day to maintain their weight in a tropical climate. The same result could be achieved by allowing a bird to gorge to full capacity once every 3 days. Probably a wild Harpy might feed on average about twice a week, but could fast 10-14 days if necessary.

Seen in the field, the Harpy is unmistakeable by reason of its size. In flight, the wings are broad but relatively short, and the tail long; it travels with a few flaps alternating with glides, like a giant Goshawk or Sparrowhawk. Young birds go through a gradual sequence of plumage changes, and evidently do not assume fully adult feathering until at least 5 years old.

Despite their size Harpy Eagles
display great speed and agility in
pursuit of prey through the forest.

The Harpy Eagle is confined to primary forests in the New World tropics.

HARPYOPSIS NOVAEGUINEAE

Large size and pale underparts and banded tail distinguish this from other New Guinea birds of prey.

Were it not eclipsed in size and striking plumage by its close relative, the Philippine Eagle, this would rank as one of the world's most spectacular eagles. Both are believed to be related, rather more distantly, to the true Harpy Eagle, and the Guyanan Crested Eagle of South America. Though still widely distributed in New Guinea, it is threatened by habitat destruction and direct persecution. Unfortunately, a large part of its population inhabits lowland forest, which is at present subject to rapid clearance. A habitat in which it is still frequently encountered is the beech forest on the lower mountains, between 6,500 and 9,800 feet, but even here it is not safe. Its wing and tail feathers are greatly valued by New Guinea highlanders for use in head-dresses. Large numbers are killed, and sold in markets to supply these, and consequently it is rapidly disappearing from the more accessible regions.

Although still not infrequently seen by ornithologists in New Guinea, the life and habits of this eagle are very sketchily known. Partly this must be due to the very difficult terrain on the island, but partly also to the quite exceptional interest of so much of its other avifauna! Seen overhead, the New Guinea Eagle appears rather pale, with lightly barred flight feathers, whitish wing linings and a long, barred tail. Its wings are rather short and broad, in their proportions not dissimilar to those of the Philippine Eagle. Immature birds are browner above than adults, and somewhat barred on the underparts.

Soaring above the forest is the usual situation in which the New Guinea Eagle is glimpsed, but it is also sometimes sighted perched in a tall forest tree, and possibly this is one of its regular hunting stratagems. Records of food are few, but tree kangaroos, wallabies and piglets are certainly included. If watched at one of these tree perches, it may often be seen craning its head about at odd angles as it peers through the foliage in search of prey. It has been suggested that the erected ruff aids hearing by gathering sounds, rather like the facial discs of owls and harriers. The New Guinea Eagle has long legs, and these doutbless aid it when it descends to the ground, on which it can move with surprising speed and agility, holding its wings slightly raised and half open.

One nest described held a single young one when found. It was situated 65 feet up in a tree, composed of sticks, and said by local people to be used every year. Other accounts speak of nests placed high in the largest trees of the cloud forest.

Deforestation in New Guinea threatens the dwindling population of this eagle.

Demand for the decorative wing and tail feathers has led to the persecution of this bird.

T. BOYER 81.

15 PHILIPPINE EAGLE

PITHECOPHAGA JEFFERYI

All plumage similar

Immense size and rectangular wing outline are characteristics

Opposite: The deep bill and facial ruff lend the Philippine Eagle an imposing appearance.

Long known as the Monkey-eating Eagle, the new name of this bird reflects a recently awakened national pride in one of the Philippines' most magnificent wild creatures. This has come none too soon, for it is also one of the rarest and most severely threatened of the world's eagles. Extensive deforestation is the major factor which has brought its numbers so perilously low, but hunting and illicit trade in live specimens have also played their part. At last, a major conservational effort is under way; protection of suitable areas of forest and captive breeding for release to the wild are hoped to check its decline, while detailed studies of its life and habits now in progress should yield vital information for its management in the future. Mindanao is evidently its stronghold, but a recent survey suggests that more may still survive on some of the other islands than had previously been thought.

The old name of the bird was not merely bad propaganda (for to European ears, at least, the eating of monkeys has a rather sinister ring to it), but rather inaccurate, for monkeys play only a minor role in the diet. Flying lemurs are apparently the major prey, but deer, large birds such as hornbills, and even snakes are also taken. Typical habitat for the Philippine Eagle is the dense forest which clothes the slopes of the numerous volcanos in the archipelago. A regular hunting technique is to soar to a great height to reach the high peaks, then glide down over the forest canopy, seeking prey on the way. Alternatively, still hunting from a high perch is often employed.

The forested slopes of volcanos provide sanctuary for the remaining pairs of Philippine Eagles.

Like most eagles this species keeps the nest lined with fresh greenery throughout the nesting cycle.

Relatively few nests of the Philippine Eagle have been found and studied, so we are still uncertain of some of the basic facts of its breeding biology. Nests are situated high up in tall trees, and two observed recently had been sited so that they were partly hidden by creeper; possibly this is a regular habit, and it does not help in the search for a nest! Only a single egg is laid, probably usually about November, so that the young bird fledges during the dry season about April or May. The incubation period seems to be about 60 days. As with many other eagles, the parents frequently bring fresh green sprays to line the nest both during and after incubation. At one nest observed, the female performed about 70 per cent of this duty, and most of the task of brooding the young one while small. By the age of 3 weeks, the eaglet weighs about 1 lb and by 5 the first feathers have appeared. Wing flapping begins about 6 weeks, and at 9, the young bird is fully feathered. The one recorded fledging period was about 105 days. Throughout incubation, the male fed the female, and also brought most of the food for the young one. Feeding by the parents continues for some time after it has fledged, and by radio telemetry of a young bird it has been determined that it stays in its parents home range for at least 1½ years. Probably, in view of the protracted period of care, the Philippine Eagles only breeds every other year – another factor making it extremely vulnerable to persecution.

Usually, the Philippine Eagle is seen in flight, either soaring, or moving between forest perches. At such times its huge size, broad rounded wings and long tail make it easy to recognize. Size, and the very deep bill are characteristic when it is perched, though the crest is not always obvious, unless raised in response to mobbing birds, or the presence of another raptor. The usual call is a thin scream, sounding rather feeble from such an impressive bird. Shorter, repeated notes are sometimes given when the eagle is excited.

Charles Lindbergh, the pioneer aviator, was one of the first to sound a warning about the plight of this splendid eagle. Let us hope that the fight to save it is not too late, and that future generations will still be able to see the bird he admired so much soaring above the forested slopes of the Philippine Islands.

ICTINAETUS MALAYENSIS

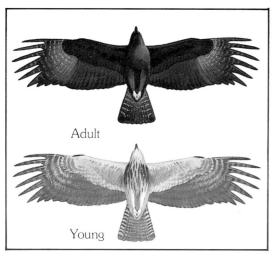

Adult

Young

Exceptionally long wings with flight feathers widely splayed at the tips produce an unmistakeable flight silhouette.

Unique among eagles in structure and way of life, this fascinating bird inhabits forested mountain country from India through South-east Asia to Sulawesi and the Moluccas. Although the main features of its life and habits are known, it is surprising that so strange a species has not yet been the subject of a really detailed study. It is hoped that the habitats on which it depends will escape deforestation long enough to enable such research to take place.

The Indian Black Eagle is not at all closely related to the Black Eagle of Africa, and is generally thought to have affinities with the Booted and Bonelli's Eagles: alternatively, some ornithologists suggest a relationship with kites. From all of these, however, it is distinguished by its highly specialized wings and feet. The former are remarkable for the very long flexible primaries, which splay out widely in flight to give a distinctive silhouette. Even more unusual, the feet have the outer toe greatly reduced in length, while the talons on the rest are exceptionally long, but much less curved than in other eagles.

When the eagle is seen hunting, some of the reasons for its structural peculiarities become clearer. Its usual strategy is to soar in wide circles over the forest at an unusually slow pace, its wings motionless and angled slightly upwards. Almost certainly the long, splayed primaries are an aerodynamic device allowing it to maintain a very low airspeed without stalling; coupled with this, the body size is very small in relation to wing area, giving it exceptionally low wing loading. Endowed with this ability to fly slowly, it can inspect the forest minutely, and circle in and out of small gaps in the canopy, seeking lizards, small mammals and birds, but above all, eggs and nestlings. These may be snatched out of the nest, but the Black Eagle will also take the entire structure, from

This eagle regularly snatches young birds and sometimes the whole nest from tree top sites. Immatures have pale streaks and spots.

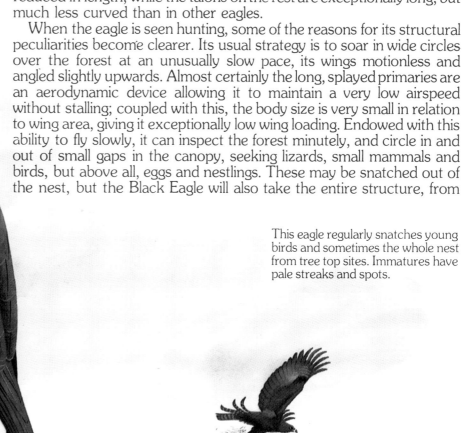

The right foot of this eagle shows the reduced outer toe and unusually straight talons.

Opposite: Even at rest the great length of the wings is apparent.

which the contents can be removed at leisure. Probably this habit provides some explanation for the peculiar structure of the feet. Unconfirmed native reports even credit the bird with the ability to snatch young monkeys from their mothers.

Despite its adaptations for leisurely flight, the Indian Black Eagle can muster a turn of speed when necessary. Sometimes this is seen when it drops suddenly onto a victim in the treetops or even the forest floor, but more strikingly when it enters the mouths of caves to take bats or swiftlets – a skill in which it rivals the even more specialized Bat Hawk. The display flights are still more spectacular, involving high speed dives of 9,800 feet or more, with wings completely folded, ending with an upward swoop. Pairs also perform chases among the forest trees, threading their way around them with ease and skill.

Breeding appears to take place mainly during the dry season in areas where this is well marked, though in truly tropical areas it is likely to be more irregular. The nest is not often found, even in areas where it is certain that the bird breeds. In general it seems usually to be sited high in a large tree, often one overgrown with creepers, or overhanging a precipice. Small sticks form the bulk of the nest, which is up to 4 feet across. In the center is a depression lined with thick green leaves from creepers or oaks. One, or rarely 2 eggs are laid, usually whitish in ground color with rich brown blotching and a few black or gray spots. Details of the role of the sexes during incubation and fledging, and the duration of each are unknown. However, both parents are very active and aggressive in defense of the nest, and at such times may utter a croaking call. Other than this, the Indian Black Eagle is usually silent, though rarely a shrill cry may be given, in flight or perched.

The Indian Black Eagle is a skilled hunter of bats.

T. BOYER 81.

Limestone caves with their huge bat
colonies provide attractive hunting
areas for this Eagle.

17 SPOTTED EAGLE

AQUILA CLANGA

Adult

Young

In flight wings appear broader and more square cut than those of the Lesser Spotted Eagle.

Adults lack the bold spotting of the immature.

Usually it is the juvenile and immature stages of birds of prey which are difficult to identify, but in this eagle they are easier. Indeed it is the immature Spotted Eagle which gives its name to the whole species, for adult birds entirely lack the bold pale spots on the upperparts and wing coverts. Confusion is most likely with the Lesser Spotted Eagle, but young birds of this species have paler upperparts, with white bars on secondaries and greater coverts, but otherwise unspotted. Moreover, in the young Spotted Eagle flying overhead, the underwing coverts appear darker than the flight feathers; the reverse is true in the Lesser Spotted Eagle. Adults are a good deal more difficult to separate, but those of the Spotted Eagle appear generally darker, particularly on the head, producing a more marked contrast with the pale base of the bill. Overhead, the darkness of the underwing coverts may still be noticeable, but adult Spotted Eagles in flight are perhaps best recognized by their silhouette, with broader wings which are square cut across the rather drooping primaries creating an effect likened to a "ragged mat." The head and tail also appear relatively smaller than in the Lesser Spotted Eagle, further emphasizing the breadth of the wings. A pale form occurs which could be confused with a Steppe or Tawny Eagle, but still shows the distinctive flight silhouette.

Most lowland forests, preferably near water, are the breeding habitat of the Spotted Eagle, while even in its winter quarters, this migratory species prefers marshy areas, often near the coast. Due to its choice of habitat, it has probably always been a scattered and thinly spread species, and consequently its decline has been relatively unnoticed and poorly documented. Nevertheless, it has over the past century diminished from a scarce European breeding bird to a very rare one. Most of its existing population now is spread over a wide area of the Asian USSR. The numbers involved, and their status and future prospects can scarcely be conjectured, but it is difficult to feel optimistic.

The Spotted Eagle is an efficient, if unspectacular general hunter and scavenger, preying mainly on small to medium sized mammals including voles, hamsters, marmots and ground squirrels. Some birds are taken, ranging from sparrows to young rooks or herons snatched from colonies. Waterbirds such as ducks and coots are often captured; the latter is attacked by first isolating an individual from a flock, then persistently stooping as it surfaces between dives until successful. Reptiles and amphibians are taken where plentiful, including grass snakes, and even fish have been recorded as prey. Some insects are eaten, and in Africa it is attracted to locust swarms as well as to bush fires. It may harry other birds to rob them of prey, and will take carrion readily.

Territories are usually quite large, roughly 25-35 sq miles and nests widely dispersed, although 4 pairs in an area of 15 acres have been recorded. Displays commence soon after the territory is re-occupied, and include high-circling by both birds together, often rising to great heights. The male may plunge with half folded wings towards the female soaring below. The nest is usually placed in a large tree, at heights up to 80 feet but where trees are unavailable may be in a large bush as low as 10 feet. Nests are re-used year after year, enlarging from an original diameter of about 2½ feet to 3½ feet wide and 3¼ feet deep. The shallow cup is lined with green leaves and grass, added throughout the nesting

Immature in flight

cycle. Both sexes build, but incubation is carried out entirely by the female, and lasts 42-44 days. One to 3 (usually 1) eggs form the clutch, but only occasionally are 2 young successfully reared. They are tended and fed by the female at first, and probably both parents hunt towards the end of the fledging period. The duration of this is from 60-65 days, and the young attain independence after 20-30 days.

Outside the breeding season, many Spotted Eagles, particularly more northern breeders, migrate south. A few of these birds remain in Europe, wintering in the Balkans, northern Italy and the South of France; stragglers have occurred in Britain and Ireland. The majority travel further, however, to winter quarters stretching across the northern tropics of Africa, the Middle East, India and China. The exact range limits and numbers involved in winter are very imperfectly known, due to extensive confusion with the Lesser Spotted Eagle. On migration, Spotted Eagles travel singly, in pairs, or in parties up to 5 or 6. In Africa, large numbers are sometimes seen at locust swarms or grass fires.

The Spotted Eagle prefers forested areas near water during the breeding season.

Young Spotted Eagles nearly ready to fly show the bold buff spotting that gives the species its name.

18 STEPPE EAGLE

AQUILA RAPAX

The broad pale band across the centre of the wing makes flying immatures easier to identify than adult birds.

The immature Steppe Eagle shows pale bars across wings and back.

Quite the most confusing of eagles, even the names of this species require explanation. The appellation "Steppe Eagle" refers strictly speaking to the Eurasian races. A.r. oreintalis and A.r. nipalensis, the latter having a more easterly distribution. However, 3 other geographical races are recognized, all generally known as "Tawny Eagles". These are A.r. rapax of central and southern Africa, A.r. belisarius of North Africa and A.r. vindhiana of India. These various races differ greatly in size and overall color, with the serious risk of confusion with other eagles. This account is concerned mainly with the Steppe Eagles proper, which average a good deal larger and darker than the other races. As with the Spotted and Lesser Spotted Eagles, young birds are easier to identify than adults: their distinctive feature is shown in flight – a broad whitish band across the centre of the underwing. Flight is heavy, lacking the buoyancy of the Golden Eagle; a closer resemblance is to the Imperial Eagle, A. heliaca. The Steppe Eagle spends much more time on low perches, or even on the ground, than its relatives; these habits cause a good deal of wear and tear which is often obvious from the state of the plumage.

The Steppe Eagle, as its name indicates, is primarily a bird of open country (although Tawny Eagles in northwest Africa inhabit forested mountains), its distribution embracing most of the lowland middle latitudes of Eurasia from which the Golden Eagle is absent. It seems to prefer arid areas, and unlike the Spotted Eagle, avoids the vicinity of marshes and inland waters. In winter quarters the Steppe Eagle occurs especially on open grassland with scattered trees and termite colonies. It is a versatile hunter and scavenger, able to capture a wide variety of prey, but not above robbing other birds or visiting carcasses to eat carrion. On its Eurasian breeding grounds, it specializes in taking ground squirrels and hares, but many other small to medium mammals are recorded, including hedgehogs, jerboas, voles, marmots, weasels and polecats. Birds are less frequent prey, but include bustards, partridges, quail and lapwings. Some snakes and lizards are eaten, as well as locusts and carrion. In some parts of the USSR saiga carcasses resulting from overhunting or birth accidents are a major food source. In African winter quarters, the list is more extensive still, with mammals ranging from shrews to dik-diks (small antelopes), genets and hyraxes. There seems to be a tendency for adults and immatures to differ in their winter diet and habits, the former foraging alone for vertebrate prey and carrion, while the younger birds often gather in numbers to feed on localized food concentrations such as termites, weaver bird nestlings or mole-rat colonies. In Eurasia, it hunts largely from soaring flight at 500-600 feet, but will wait by burrows to catch rodents as they emerge, or will walk about seeking prey. In Africa, the chief hunting techniques are short flights between perches, still hunting, or skimming flight low over the ground. Immatures seeking termite swarms follow weather movements to settle for a time in areas where rains are just beginning – conditions which trigger the emergence of the insects. Food piracy appears to be confined to the winter quarters; species recorded as being robbed of prey range from kestrels and black-winged kites up to such imposing raptors as Martial Eagles and Lammergeiers. It is also capable of driving vultures and marabous away from a carcass, though preferring to let them do the initial butchery.

T. BOYER 81.

Head of a Steppe Eagle showing the characteristically flat face

Northern populations are named after the steppes of Central Asia in which they are still to be found.

Due to their migratory habits, Steppe Eagles probably pair only seasonally, though the more sedentary Tawny Eagles may have longer lasting pair bonds. Pair formation may occur during spring migration, and doubtless there are displays and rituals on the Eurasian breeding grounds, but most of our information for the species relates to the Tawny Eagles of Africa and India. High-circling, alone or as a pair occurs, but although the male stoops around the female, she usually does not respond by rolling or presenting her talons as in some other related eagles. An undulating "sky-dance" has also been reported.

Nesting habits differ considerably from those of other Aquila eagles as a consequence of the Steppe Eagle's predilection for open country where few trees are to be found. A low hillock or cairn, a ruined building, haystack or a low bush will suffice to accommodate a large flat nest 3 feet or more in diameter, though little more than 12 inches deep when new. There may be several nests used in rotation, but individual nests may also be re-used repeatedly. Branches, with some animal bones form the bulk of the nest which is lined with grass, straw or fur. Both birds build, the male concentrating on delivering material while the female assembles it. One to 3 eggs are laid and the female incubates them, probably for about 45 days. She tends them while small, the male bringing food, but probably both hunt later in the fledging period. The duration of fledging is uncertain. It has been estimated at 60 days for the Steppe Eagle, yet for 76-85 days in the Tawny Eagle. This discrepancy seems altogether too great to credit, and clearly more study of all populations and races is required. The ratio of young fledged to eggs hatched is not known, but apparently at least some die as a result of aggression between siblings. After fledging we know very little for Steppe Eagles, though Tawny Eagles are reputed to be independent after about 6 weeks. However, juvenile Tawny Eagles sometimes stay with a parent until the next breeding season.

19 IMPERIAL EAGLE

AQUILA HELIACA

The Imperial Eagle appears heavier and less graceful on the wing than the Golden Eagle.

Adults of the Eastern race have white restricted to the shoulders.

Slightly smaller than the Golden Eagle on average, but more strikingly marked, the Imperial Eagle is one of Europe's most impressive birds of prey, and at the same time, one of the most severely threatened. This is in part a consequence of its habitat choice. Unlike the Golden Eagle it seems to shun mountainous areas in most parts of its range, although it is occasionally found in them in regions where its relative does not occur. Its preferred habitat instead seems to be parkland or Steppe country, with scattered trees or small woods intermingled with open grassland, marshes or even cultivation. Obviously, in such areas it comes more into conflict with man, and is at the same time more accessible to persecution. Increasingly, at the present time, it is also being affected by pollution and habitat deterioration. Overhead wires, for instance, take their toll; 3 were killed by colliding with them in 1975 alone in the Coto Doñana.

Two different races of the Imperial Eagle occur, once considered separate species. The Iberian race is the better known, and has been the subject of a detailed study of behaviour. It is also the more striking of the two, with extensive white patches on the shoulders, and along the leading edge of the wing. In the Eastern race, the white patches are restricted to the shoulders, and are less extensive. Adults of both races resemble the Golden Eagle in general appearance, apart from the white patches on the shoulder, but immatures differ considerably from young Goldens, and might more easily be confused with young Steppe Eagles. They lack the white tail base of the immature Golden, having instead a rufous-brown one, and have pale buff spotting on the upperparts. They can always be distinguished by the combination of large size and heavily streaked underparts. Immatures of the Iberian race are rather more rufous above than those of the Eastern, and have the streaking on the underparts largely confined to the breast region. The Imperial Eagle is much more vocal than the Golden, especially during the breeding season; a deep barking call is the commonest utterance, but many others are recorded, especially as part of displaying and between members of a pair.

Though its powers of flight are considerable, the Imperial Eagle lacks the great speed and manoeuvrability of the Golden, and rarely takes birds in the air. It hunts both by spending long periods of time perched on vantage points and by soaring. A great variety of prey have been recorded, ranging from animals the size of voles up to hares and geese, but most are fairly large. For the Iberian race, rabbits and hares are important prey, while the Eastern race favors the ground squirrel or suslik. Items of carrion recorded include goats, lambs, and even a stranded dolphin. Other prey include a wide range of rodents, birds (predominantly ground and water birds, but also various passerines and even other birds of prey), and a few reptiles, including snakes. Food requirements have been calculated at 14-21 oz per day for the Eastern race and 9-10 oz per day for the slightly smaller Iberian race. However up to 42 oz may sometimes be taken in a day.

Imperial Eagles exhibit a strong pair bond, and in migratory populations it is observed that members of a pair will travel together. The species is not gregarious in other ways, however, and groups or parties are rarely seen. Aerial displays are frequent and spectacular. A high circling display, with mock attacks and talon presentation seems

Opposite: The white shoulder and wing edges lend this eagle a handsome and distinctive appearance.

The plains of the Coto Doñana are one of the last strongholds of this species in Western Europe.

the most usual, with occasional talon grasping and cartwheeling, and there is also an undulating "sky-dance" like that of other members of the genus Aquila. One individual may perform the high circling display, while the other is engaged in the sky dance. During the latter, loud calls are given in the diving phases of the flight. Spectacular aerobatics are also recorded during territorial conflicts.

Within favorable habitat, nests are generally spaced $\frac{1}{4}$ to 1 mile apart, though they may be closer together where sites are limited. The nest is a typical eagle structure of large sticks, lined with smaller twigs, grass and fur. It is placed in a large tree 33-80 feet up but occasionally in low bushes where there are no trees, and very rarely on a cliff ledge. As with other eagles, sprays of fresh greenery are added throughout the nesting cycle. A new nest averages 4-6 feet in diameter and 2-2$\frac{1}{4}$ feet in depth, increasing to perhaps 9 feet wide by 6 deep with repeated use. Both sexes build, the female taking the greater share, and a new nest may be completed in as little as 10 days.

The usual clutch is 2-3 eggs, sometimes 1 or 4. Incubation starts with the first egg, and lasts 43 days per egg. Both sexes incubate, the male taking a substantial share, but not provisioning his mate regularly – a different system from that in most other Aquila eagles, and so far only demonstrated in the Iberian race. The female appears to dominate the male at the eyrie, sometimes taking food away from him and greeting him with a rather menacing ritual, calling with wings hanging from the shoulders, then jerked back and up 5 or 6 times, repeated at intervals of 10-15 seconds. This may put the male off from visiting the nest at all. In the case of a pair photographed in the Coto Doñana by Eric Hosking and Guy Mountfort, the male brought food to a tree 275 yards away, from which the female was obliged to fetch it.

T. BOYER 81.

The immature can be distinguished from that of the Golden Eagle by its streaky underparts.

A bird of the Eastern race quartering open country in search of ground squirrels, a favorite prey.

The young are brooded continuously for the first 7 days after hatching, mainly by the female, and during the next 10 days, the period of brooding decreases to about half the day. Both parents feed the young, the male doing most of the hunting for the first few weeks. It appears that disputes between the siblings are less frequent and less intense than in other species of Aquila; 2 are often reared, and sometimes 3. In broods of 2, even where both are the same size, 1 always becomes dominant over the other, but usually a brief threat is enough to drive the subordinate member away from the food. In a brood of 3, the dominant chick bullied one of similar size to itself, but the smallest one was left in peace. An additional reason why the young seem to survive together better than in other eagles may be that the parent Imperial Eagles continue to share out food among them for a longer period than in most of their relatives. The chicks are always very noisy in the presence of their parents, even when their crops are full; they will beg enthusiastically when an adult merely brings a branch to the nest. They begin to perform the mantling display over food received from about 37 days. Fledging takes places after 65-77 days, and the young remain in the vicinity of the nest for a further 2-3 weeks. They may stay with their parents throughout the following winter. The age of total independence is not known, nor the age of first breeding; however, adult plumage is not assumed until the birds are 4-5 years old.

Although reasonable populations still exist in some areas, the Imperial Eagle is a seriously endangered species, at least in the western palaearctic part of its range. The Iberian race is virtually confined to Spain, where 60 pairs were estimated to survive in 1977. In the east, rapidly declining populations exist in Czechoslovakia (10-15 pairs), Hungary (8-10 pairs), Yugoslavia, Bulgaria and Greece (10-12 pairs). In Rumania, the situation is slightly better, despite a marked decrease, some 100-120 pairs were believed to exist in 1977. Reliable figures are not available for the USSR but there, too, the species is in decline. Some 50-99 pairs are thinly spaced out in northern Turkey, and a few survive in Cyprus. Clearly, only stringent protection and a major conservational effort can hope to halt the decline before it is too late.

20 GOLDEN EAGLE

AQUILA CHRYSAETOS

As the most numerous and widespread large eagle in the Northern Hemisphere with four races currently recognized, the Golden Eagle has probably acquired a more voluminous literature than any other species. Despite its high world population, however, it is severely threatened and persecuted in many parts of its range, and despite all that has been written about it, there are still aspects of its life and habits which remain poorly understood.

Deliberate persecution arises mainly from two human activities – game preservation and sheep farming. In Scotland, it is on grouse moors that the eagle encounters its worst enemies, for it is tolerated or even encouraged in deer forest. Gin traps, poisoned bait or simply the shotgun are still employed by unscrupulous keepers, unable or unwilling to admit the negligible effect the eagle has on grouse numbers, while many shepherds still fear depredations on lambs, despite a mass of evidence to the contrary. In North America, livestock again provides the motive, but the killing has been on a vaster scale, with eagles pursued and shot from airplanes. In Britain today, however, the greatest threats may be side effects of human activities having no harmful intent at all. Golden Eagles are shy and wary birds, for all their size and power, and are easily disturbed at the nest.

More such conflicts of interest will doubtless arise, and it may be that publicity rather than secrecy is the answer; the ospreys of Loch Garten have survived nearly 1,000,000 visitors in two decades with careful management by the Royal Society for the Protection of Birds, and a similar system of controlled access and viewing points has been suggested by Leslie Brown for Golden Eagle eyries threatened by the human leisure explosion. A more sinister threat appeared in the 1970s, when a sequence of breeding failures in Scotland was traced to the use of dieldrin in sheep dips, finding its way into the eagles' diet via carrion. A ban on the use of this chemical appears to have led to an improvement, but continual monitoring of breeding success is essential to provide early warning of similar dangers which may arise in the future.

The situation elsewhere in Europe has been summarized in considerable detail by Maarten Bijleveld. Scotland and Switzerland emerge as the only two countries in which the species is even reasonably secure, in both cases due to well enforced protection laws. In Scandinavia, where there are huge expanses of suitable habitat, the Golden Eagle has declined very significantly this century. At Falsterbo, in south Sweden, where birds of prey pass in great numbers during autumn migration, it was formerly possible to see as many as 10 or 20 in a day during times of peak passage; now it is seldom seen there at all. A factor which appears to have weighed against it very severely is the belief of many Lapps that the bird kills reindeer. This probably arises from the plentiful supply of carrion that becomes available in early summer, when the receding snows expose the frozen corpses of many reindeer that die during the harsh winter. Eagles frequently feed on these, but are unfortunately often assumed to have killed the beasts which they are seen eating, and are heavily persecuted as a result. In Germany the Golden Eagle virtually disappeared as a breeder during the eighteenth century. Today, it survives only in the Bavarian Alps, where perhaps 10 or so pairs may still breed annually, but breeding success is poor, and losses high. In France, reductions of 60 per cent or more have been

Chick: In four out of five broods where two young hatch, there is only one survivor.

Adult

Young

Long wings and majestic flight
distinguish the Golden Eagle from
smaller sized species in its range.

Opposite: The Golden Eagle's powers
of flight enable it to patrol large areas
of mountainous country effortlessly.

estimated in various regions since the Second World War; today, the
best population, of some 14-18 pairs, is probably that in the Basses Alpes
and Alpes Maritimes, while a few pairs also survive in Corsica. For many
other countries data is insufficient, but tends to give the same picture, of
a declining and threatened, though not yet critically low, population of
eagles.

The onslaught against Golden Eagles in the western USA has been
well documented by Seton Gordon. It has been most severe in west
Texas, in areas where sheep farming is intensively pursued, and there
seems little doubt that in this region at least, eagle predation on lambs
can be considerable. This is doubtless because the drastic alteration in
land use here has left little else for the eagles; it remains a general rule
that the birds will rarely bother to kill lambs as long as natural prey
remain abundant. Airplanes have played a crucial role in persecution of
Golden Eagles in Texas and California. A number of pilots have
specialized in eagle hunting, and are ready to take to the air at a
moment's notice when a rancher telephones to report an eagle sighting.
The standard weapon is a sawn-off shotgun, aimed and fired quickly
during a brief interval in which the pilot takes both hands off the
controls. Clearly this calls for nerve and skill, but it is hard for any
conservationist to appreciate these qualities when the toll they result in
is considered. One well-known hunter during the decade following the
Second World War average about 1,000 eagles killed per year, and
several others have closely approached this figure. It seems clear that to
achieve such figures, the birds killed must have been drawn from a large
area, and probably many were birds from mountains well to the south
over the Mexican border.

Prose – and verse – written about the Golden Eagle during the
nineteenth century and later tends to dwell on the spectacular,
especially the size of the bird's prey. Present day attitudes may seem
more prosaic, but lead to a better understanding of the bird's ecology.
Looked at objectively, it is obviously desirable that the usual prey
tackled should be of a size that can be carried off whole after killing;
although larger prey can be dismembered, it is likely that other
scavengers will have their fill before the eagle returns for more. A
Golden Eagle in calm conditions can only rise and fly easily with a little
over 2 lbs though when flying against a strong wind up to six times this
weight can be carried for a short distance. Thus, brown hares, weighing
up to 9 lbs are the largest prey regularly taken in Scotland, while grouse,
another frequent victim, weigh only $1\frac{1}{4}$-$1\frac{1}{2}$ lbs. Weights of the Eagles
themselves range from just under $6\frac{1}{2}$ lbs in small males to over 13 lbs in
some large females. Victims occasionally include other predators, such
as foxes, stoats and mink, and Seton Gordon quotes an eye witness
account of an attack on a wildcat. This last, however, led to the death of
both the eagle and its intended prey. Although very large prey are
sometimes killed, including apparently roe-deer calves and even
pronghorn antelope, such cases are exceedingly rare, and ecologically
irrelevant. More important is the overall food intake, and for this we
have good figures, derived from captive birds, and supported by field
studies. Leslie Brown and Adam Watson have estimated that a pair of
adults, rearing an average brood, plus any unattached birds in the home
range, would require about 600 lbs of prey per year, including about 20-

Glens and mountains typified by the
Scottish Highlands are the preferred
habitat throughout the Golden
Eagle's range.

Head: The golden hackles on the nape and neck, which give the species its name, are characteristic of adult birds.

Most prey is taken on the ground.

30 per cent which would be wasted (e.g. by loss to other scavengers). Of this total, roughly 110 lbs would be carrion, 200 lbs mammals, and 160 lbs birds, though proportions would vary a good deal from place to place.

Large prey animals are the rule, rather than the exception, when the eagle is used for falconry. Fortunately, it has never been a popular bird with European falconers, or pressure on its remaining populations there would be even greater. Its use for this purpose has been practised mainly by Mongol peoples in the mountainous regions bordering Kirghiz and Sinkiang, and certainly persisted well into the present century, perhaps even to the present time. The birds used are of the race A.c. daphanea, which is larger and more powerful than those of Britain and Europe. They are taken from the eyrie when feathered, and training starts immediately, as with other falconer's birds, by accustoming it to eat from the hand. This is followed by training it to attack a lure – usually a stuffed fox skin – dragged along the ground. Finally, caged animals are released for it to pursue.

When hunting with an eagle, the falconer is usually on horseback, and takes the weight of the bird on a prop resting on the knees or saddle. It is carried on the right arm, contrary to the usual practice of European falconers. A leather hood covers its head until prey is sighted. Its principal quarry is the corsac fox, whose pelts are of considerable value; consequently the birds must learn to kill efficiently, with minimum damage to the skin. As soon as a fox is captured, the bird is taken off it and fed on pieces of meat carried by its handler. Hares and gazelles are also pursued with eagles, and in some areas wolves. In the latter case, an outright kill is obviously a rare event; instead, the eagle grips the animal's muzzle with one foot, to prevent it biting, and its back with the other, holding it until its handler catches up to dispatch it with knife or rifle. Although many of these formidable adversaries have been killed with the aid of eagles, the struggle is often a severe one, and occasionally an eagle is killed. An epic tale is recounted by Seton Gordon of an exceptionally large and fierce wolf in Kirghiz which killed eleven eagles before itself falling victim to the twelfth. For this feat, the falconer was rewarded with a gold medal personally presented by Stalin! Doubtless some exaggeration is to be expected in such stories, but in general hunting wolves with eagles seems well corroborated.

In one aspect of its life, the Golden Eagle well merits sensational prose; it is superb in flight, combining a capability for speed rivalling that of the peregrine with the ability to soar effortlessly on updraughts or thermals, or to quarter a hillside as slowly as a harrier. Such abilities are demanded by its choice of mountainous habitat, and are matched (indeed exceeded) only by the Black or Verreaux Eagle of Africa which inhabits similar terrain. When moving across country, a frequent technique is to soar high over a ridge, then glide downwards at great speed to traverse a valley. Although most prey are taken on the ground the Golden Eagle is fully capable of intercepting grouse or other birds in flight, sometimes stooping at them falcon style. Displays resemble those of other eagles, with an undulating series of alternate dives and upward swoops the commonest, but they are performed with exceptional speed and skill. During displays, mewing calls may be uttered, but the Golden Eagle is generally a silent bird at other times.

GOLDEN EAGLE

Golden Eagles are not strongly territorial birds, and seem to space themselves out without resorting to frequent conflict over boundaries as occurs in some other species of eagle, and many smaller raptors. Consequently, the area in which a pair regularly lives and hunts is better called a "home range" than a territory. The birds mate for life, though when one dies, the survivor is usually quick to find a new mate. Within the home range are situated from 1-11 nests, all of which have new material added from time to time, though often only one or two are used for breeding. These traditional eyries are often of great antiquity, for records of some of them extend back to the turn of the century or earlier, far longer than the lifetimes of the birds which have inhabited them. Length of life, indeed, has been another focal point for myths and tall stories; despite tales of centenarian eagles, Leslie Brown estimates 18 years as the average span in the world, deduced from data on breeding rate. In captivity, ages of 40-45 years have been recorded.

Refurbishing of the chosen nest takes place mainly during February and March. Its foundation is of sticks, with softer material such as grass and woodrush added as a lining. In common with many other raptors, the birds bring fresh green sprays to the nest shortly before laying, sometime during the first 3 weeks of March. The eggs are usually 2 in number (rarely 3 or 4), and are laid 3 or 4 days apart. Incubation, lasting about 44 days, begins with the first egg, so that the young hatch several days apart, each roughly the weight of a blackbird at birth. Early in their lives the "Cain and Abel" battle characteristics of eagles occurs. Golden Eagles are relatively unusual in that about a fifth of younger nestlings survive; in many other eagle species destruction of the smaller siblings is complete. About 80 days elapse before the eaglet or eaglets make a first flight; thereafter, the young show an attachment to their birthplace which gradually wanes during their first winter. The few Scottish ringing recoveries so far available indicate a pattern of short-range dispersal by young birds similar to that in, e.g., the buzzard, but eagles nesting far north in Scandinavia must be prepared for a long migration soon after the breeding season has concluded. Immature birds up to their second year can be readily distinguished from adults by the large areas of white at the base of the tail and near the carpal joint of the wing.

Immature birds show white at the base of the tail.

21 WEDGE-TAILED EAGLE

AQUILA AUDAX

Adult

Young

The long wedge-shaped tail makes this eagle unmistakable in flight.

A fondness for carrion makes the Wedge-tailed Eagle an easy victim for poisoning.

Australia's largest and most impressive raptor, the Wedge-tailed Eagle could just as well have been a national bird as America's Bald Eagle. Such status, however, has been little protection to the symbol of the New World, and doubtless would have availed no better in defending the Wedge-tail against the persecution it has suffered – more intense, probably, than any other eagle. The fact that it survives is testimony to the large proportion of Australia's area which remains wilderness.

Lambs are, of course, the excuse given for waging war against the Wedge-tail Eagle, despite the evidence from careful study that live ones are rarely taken. Sober fact, however, counts for little where stories that eagles hunt in formations and can kill animals up to the size of horses are given credence. In one way, though, man may have helped the bird, for carrion is always readily accepted, and roads through Australian bush provide it in abundance, in the form of dead wallabies, bandicoots, or in Northern Territories even dead buffalo etc. Prior to the advent of Europeans and their animals, marsupials up to medium sized kangaroos probably provided much of the Wedge-tail's prey. Rabbits are now the most favored victim where available, followed by kangaroos and wallabies. In dry areas, reptiles such as goannas and thorny-tailed lizards may constitute an important fraction of the diet. Probably a good deal of their quarry is captured during early morning and evening, when the birds quarter their territory just above the treetops. Later in the day they may perch or soar, reaching heights of up to 6,500 feet or more, and will make long slanting dives from these levels to attack prey seen on the ground. When carrion is seen, up to 30 or 40 individuals might gather, depending on the size of the carcass. In captivity, an adult eagle requires less than 1 lb food per day.

The Wedge-tailed Eagle's liking for high soaring is exhibited to the full just before the breeding season, when the pair spend much time in the air together, and may indulge in spectacular aerobatics, including mock attacks, talon presentation and even looping the loop. Shrill whistling calls often accompany these performances. Breeding takes place during the southern spring, mainly in August or September, often earlier further north. One to 3 eggs, but usually 2, are laid. They are incubated by the female, and food is brought to her by the male. The incubation period has not been ascertained, but fledging takes some 63-70 days after hatching. The young are fully feathered at 49 days; measurements of weight at various stages indicate more rapid growth before feathering than after. The female feeds the young in the early stages, and helps them up to about 40 days old. They can fly well after 90 days, but evidently continue to be dependent on their parents for some time after this. I have seen well developed young eagles screaming insistently for food and with parents in attendance during February near Darwin, New Territories, where the breeding cycle must have started in August at least.

Opposite: Australia's most
magnificent eagle, this bird has been
intensively persecuted.

Small wallabies must have been a
major prey before the introduction of
the rabbit.

T. BOYER 80.

22 GURNEY'S EAGLE

AQUILA GURNEYI

Adult

Young

Long wings and plain coloration distinguish this from the New Guinea Eagle.

Opposite: An immature bird

Unlike the New Guinea Eagle this species prefers lowland forest. The future of this little known eagle is threatened by deforestation.

Least known member of the genus Aquila (the true eagles), Gurney's Eagle could also become the first to reach extinction. Though some of its relatives, such as the Imperial Eagle, face grave dangers, their plight is at least well known and well publicized. Gurney's Eagle tends to be forgotten, and so meagre is the information available on it that it is difficult to be sure how severe is the threat to its existence. The little we do know, leads us to fear the worst. Unlike other true Eagles, Gurney's appear to have become adapted to a forest existence, and unfortunately, the forests it prefers are lowland ones, especially near the coast. In its range, which includes the Northern Moluccas, Aru Islands and New Guinea, deforestation of coastal lowlands is at present intense. The situation is probably worst in the Indonesian parts of its range, where population growth has led to a continual demand for more land on which to grow rice. Papua New Guinea, where the traditional diet has required less land, is now expanding trade and commerce rapidly, with a consequent increased pressure on forested areas.

Gurney's Eagle is still occasionally encountered in New Guinea, but our ignorance of its habits remains almost total. It is usually seen soaring, when the dark coloration of adults, and the unbarred tail of the paler immatures should distinguish it from the New Guinea Eagle. Its wings are also proportionately longer and narrower. The Wedge-tailed Eagle may occasionally straggle to New Guinea, but its characteristic tail shape would at once distinguish it from Gurney's.

T. BOYER 81.

23 BLACK EAGLE

AQUILA VERREAUXI

Adult

Young

The unusual wing shape makes the Black Eagle easy to identify in flight.

Opposite: The Black Eagle exceeds even the Golden Eagle in its powers of flight.

Immatures show extensive pale mottling.

Though not the most powerful, or even the largest of eagles, to many ornithologists this is the supreme bird of prey, unsurpassed in its powers of flight, and truly regal in its bearing. The simple name of Black Eagle scarcely does justice to the majestic impression created by the aquiline features outlined in yellow against sable plumage. Perhaps to be preferred is the title of Verreaux's Eagle, commemorating one of two French brothers who together spent many years pioneering the natural history of the Cape region of South Africa, early in the nineteenth century.

Most observers will first encounter the Black Eagle in flight, for most of its time is spent on the wing. From below, the body appears all black, but as the bird banks, the contrasting white patch on the back may be seen. A pale area at the bases of the primaries is visible from above and below. In bad light, when none of these features can be discerned, the bird is still recognizable by the shape of the wings, which narrow towards the body, and reach maximum breadth two thirds of the way to the tip. Like the Golden Eagle of the Northern Hemisphere, which in many ways it resembles, the Black Eagle is a very silent bird. A quiet cluck, or when threatened, a sharp bark or scream are recorded, while a whistling note, "heeeee oh", is reserved for display.

Black Eagles prefer dry mountainous country, such as South Africa's Drakensberg, the plateau edges of Ethiopia, or the Matopos in Zimbabwe. In the latter country, they have been intensively studied by teams of birdwatchers co-ordinated by Carl Vernon and Valerie Gargett. Over an area of 240 sq miles they have located over 50 pairs of Black Eagles. The number probably fluctuates, but at the end of 1976, 59 pairs were known, a density of 1 pair per 4 sq miles.

Dassies (hyraxes) are the staple prey of the Black Eagle. In the Matopos study they comprised 98 per cent of the 1,892 prey items recorded. Two species of hyrax are present in the Matopos, but their frequency in the diet seems only to reflect their relative abundance, rather than any preference on the part of the eagles. They are captured by quartering the rocky hill slopes, with a quick turn and swoop to seize prey when seen. Other items recorded by the Matopos team include monkeys, small antelopes, guinea fowl, francolins and monitor lizards.

The breeding biology and population dynamics of the Black Eagle are probably better known than those of any other eagle, as a result of the Matopos survey. Before proceeding to the detailed analysis, some basic facts must be summarized. As in all eagles, the onset of breeding is marked by aerial displays. Not surprisingly, in view of this species' mastery of flight, these displays are highly spectacular, though rather surprisingly, they seem to be performed rather less often than in many eagles. They include an undulating "switch back" flight by the male, similar to that of many relatives, but also a "pendulum" version in which he swings back and forth across the same arc of sky. The male may dive at the female and grapple talons in mid-air, or the two may soar together.

Nests are made usually on cliff ledges, occasionally on trees, and are mostly highly inaccessible; the many excellent photographs that are available of this species testify to exceptional courage and enthusiasm on the part of the photographers. Fortunately, Black Eagles rarely attack human intruders, though an unusually aggressive female in the Drakensberg repeatedly swooped at photographer Jeanne Cowder,

once knocking her sprawling and ripping her sweater. Because the ledges that support them are narrow, the nests tend to spread out sideways, rather than becoming very deep; 8 feet wide and 2 feet deep is typical. A pair may maintain from 1-3 nests over a period of years. They are made of sticks and lined with sprays of green foliage, and both sexes take part in building activities, the female rather more than the male.

Two eggs are usually laid, and after being incubated for some 46 days, they hatch, usually about 3 days apart. There then ensues the usual "Cain and Abel" battle between siblings, and there is no record of more than one eaglet surviving. This is usually over inside the first 2 weeks, and after 30 days, feathers begin to appear through the down of the remaining young one. By 8 weeks, these have grown to cover the down, but a further 6 weeks must elapse before departing the nest.

The Matopos study has revealed wide annual variations in breeding rate. Over a 13 year period, the lowest proportion breeding was 46 per cent (in 1975) while the highest was 89 per cent (in 1970). Successful breeding, i.e. that resulting in fledging, fluctuated correspondingly, with lows estimated at 26-40 per cent in 1966 and 1975, and a maximum of 67 per cent in 1970. Over the whole period, 652 "pair years" resulted in 442 breeding pair years, and at most, 339 young were reared. Where it has been possible to follow the fortunes of individual pairs, these have shown as much annual variation as those of the whole population.

Analyzing these results still further, Valerie Gargett has examined various factors which might be expected to have affected breeding success. Weather is clearly a major factor, with good breeding seasons following hot dry years, and bad ones following years of above average rainfall. Despite the fact – pointed out by Peter Steyn – that 6 eyries are visible from Cecil Rhodes' grave in the Matopos, it seems that close proximity and intervisibility to nests have an adverse effect on breeding success, and are avoided where possible. Territory size as such was not correlated with breeding success, but persistent disturbance by single adults entering established territories did reduce success.

An interesting point was the discovery that a higher success rate was obtained from 2 egg clutches than single egg ones. This suggests a possible biological reason for the laying of 2 egg clutches regardless of the inevitable fratricide of one eaglet by the other which ensues. It could well be that the second egg is worth laying as a reserve in case the first fails to hatch. However, this is as yet unproven, because the fates of first laid and second laid eggs have not been followed individually. Moreover, it is possible that birds which only lay 1 egg may be in less good condition, and less fitted to rear young than those which lay 2. Reassuringly, tests carried out on 4 infertile eggs showed pesticide

Arid mountainous country is the habitat of the Black Eagle.

Rock Hyraxes or Dassies are a staple prey.

"Cain and Abel" battles between nestlings invariably result in the death of the weaker.

residues well below those found in raptor eggs in Europe and America, though in none of them were they entirely absent.

On the pessimistic side, however, the adverse impact of man is strikingly demonstrated by the contrast between results from the National Park area of the Matopos and private land on the one hand, and those from neighbouring Tribal Trust Land on the other. Eagles from areas of the first two categories raised an average of about 0.55 young per pair per year during the study period. Within the Tribal Trust Land, the average was only 0.28 young. The difference seems almost certainly due to the severe reduction in hyrax populations within the Tribal Trust Lands. This has been brought about partly by intensive hunting, and also through habitat destruction by peasant farmers and their stock. Although the farmers in the reserve do not molest the eagles – beyond occasionally taking eggs for sale to white collectors – the effect of their land use will in time be severe. Various other predators which also take hyrax are also liable to be affected; the main species concerned are Crowned Eagles, African Hawk Eagles, Wahlberg's Eagles, Cape Eagle Owls and Leopard. Although competition with these others seems to have no effect on Black Eagles under normal conditions, it may come to play a part in areas where the hyrax population has been severely reduced.

24 BONELLI'S EAGLE

HIERAETUS FASCIATUS

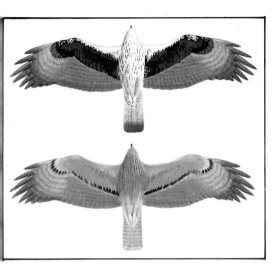

The dark band across the underside of the wing is a good field mark in flight.

Perching upright in conspicuous situations is used as territorial advertisement.

Currently, Bonelli's Eagle is regarded as a species confined to Eurasia, with a distinct race (H.f. renschi) found in the Lesser Sunda Islands of Indonesia. However, it is certainly very closely related to the African Hawk-Eagle (H. spilogaster), which has sometimes been regarded as a third race of the same species, differing in its more contrasting coloration and choice of savannah habitat. Bonelli's Eagle proper is largely confined to the Mediterranean region.

Passing quickly overhead, an adult Bonelli's Eagle might be confused with the Booted, or even an Osprey, but can be distinguished by the black band down the midline of the underwing, lack of dark patches at the wrist joint, and rather long tail. Young birds are more of a problem, but show a narrower dark band on the wing, and a pale patch at the base of the primaries. Good views are generally more difficult to obtain than with many eagles, as Bonelli's is less fond of soaring, preferring to hunt by stealth, rather like a giant Goshawk.

Although most of its prey are medium sized, Bonelli's Eagle is a bold and skilled hunter, with excellent powers of flight. A favored tactic is to wait hidden in the cover of foliage on a tree, from which it can dash out to seize prey; birds just taking off are a frequent target for such attacks. Most of its victims are taken on or near the ground, but it can catch birds in full flight, as well as snatching them from bushes or even from water on occasions. Regular hunting routes are followed each day. A pair of Bonelli's Eagles may hunt together, sometimes with one perched vertically above the other, or both in flight, one isolating a bird from a flock for the other to swoop in and kill. Prey taken by a pair is shared between them. In Europe, Redlegged Partridges and rabbits are important prey, but a wide range of other species are recorded. Birds range from larks and pigeons up to gulls and ducks, mammals from rats and gerbils up to hares. The closely related African Hawk-Eagle is recorded taking such large prey as young foxes and bush-bucks, and even another bird of prey, the Long-legged Buzzard. Lizards are quite often taken where they are plentiful, and were the main prey brought to a brood of young in Spain in a region where the rabbit population had been reduced. A seasonal shift in diet has been noted in France, with bird prey making up 80 per cent of the total from August to April, but mammals predominating from May to July.

Bonelli's Eagles are usually seen singly or in pairs, but may be found in larger numbers in situations where prey are concentrated. They are monogamous, probably pairing for life. Aerial displays occur throughout most of the year, though infrequently during the latter part of the summer. The pair together will often perform the high-circling display over the breeding locality, frequently at a great height, and very rapidly. Sometimes a branch or other object is carried during this activity, to be dropped by one bird and caught again by the other as it nears the ground. An undulating "sky-dance" is also performed, as in many other eagles; the bird dives from a great altitude, checks and rises on outstretched wings until its momentum runs out, then circles until it has regained its original height. This may be repeated as much as ten times. Melodious calls accompany the sky-dance, usually alternating short and long cries over about a minute.

Territory and nest site are strongly defended against other Bonelli's Eagles and intruders of all kinds; aggressive displays resemble those of

Wooded mountainous country is the favourite habitat of Bonelli's Eagle.

Opposite: Bonelli's Eagle is a fierce and dashing hunter of medium size prey.

the Booted Eagle. Birds of prey of other species may elicit particularly vigorous reactions, and attacks on Griffon Vultures near the nest have occasionally proved lethal as the eagles brushed their necks with talons. Leslie Brown and Peter Steyn have both experienced frightening attacks at breeding sites of the African Hawk Eagle, and the European species is quite capable of emulating it.

The nests themselves are large ones for the size of the bird, up to 6 feet wide, and after re-use, nearly as deep. They are sited on cliff ledges, trees, or occasionally on a building. The usual height range is 33-130 feet though lower ones have been recorded. The nest cup is shallow and lined with green sprays. Both sexes are involved in building, though the male's role is mainly to bring the materials needed; this may commence up to 3 or 4 months before eggs are laid. When it is at last laid, the clutch usually consists of 2 eggs, rarely 1 or 3. Both sexes incubate, but the female takes considerably the greater part; the incubation period varies from 37-40 days. The young hatch up to 48 hours apart and are brooded by one or other parent for most of their first week of life. Food is brought and fed to them for some 45 days, but the young stay with their parents for at least a further 8 weeks. Usually only 1 young one is reared, but sometimes 2. Fights between siblings are normal, but when one succumbs it is usually due to malnutrition rather than direct fratricide. The age of first breeding is not known.

Rabbits, jackdaws and lizards figure regularly in the diet of this eagle.

Immatures are browner with rufous underparts.

25 BOOTED EAGLE

HIERAETUS PENNATUS

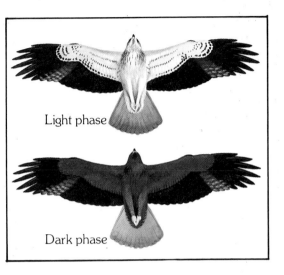
Light phase

Dark phase

Pale phase birds are mainly whitish with dark flight feathers. Dark phase birds are uniformly deep brown with a paler tail.

Birdwatchers whose travels take them to central or southern Europe know this species as one of the identification traps for those with limited experience of birds of prey. The reason is that the Booted Eagle occurs in 2 color morphs, the pale one predominating over the dark one in the ratio of 7 to 3 over much of Europe, though the proportion is more equal further east. Both are most likely to be seen in flight, when the light form is easier to identify, its pale body and underwing coverts contrasting with black flight feathers. Only the Egyptian Vulture has a similar pattern, but its silhouette is quite different. The dark morph appears mainly dark brown overhead, with a pale wedge on inner primaries and outer secondaries; it could well be confused with a Marsh Harrier or Black Kite. However, the former glides with upraised wings for much of the time, whereas the Booted Eagle soars on flat wings, while Black Kites are unmistakable once the forked tail is seen.

That the Booted Eagle can still be regularly seen at all is largely a consequence of its habitat and behavior, which make it a difficult bird to persecute directly. It is essentially a forest eagle, preferring hills and valleys of medium altitude clothed with mixed woodland and interspersed with scrub or heathland. Much of its time is spent on the wing, often at considerable altitude. Nevertheless, like other eagles, its European population is under pressure, mainly due to the steady attrition of the forests it requires.

Prey taken by the Booted Eagle are diverse, and not usually very large, but their capture often involves great speed and agility on the wing. A favorite hunting technique is to soar at a height above the forest, and when a victim is sighted, to plunge swiftly into the foliage and pursue it through the branches. A pair may hunt together, stooping in turn at a victim. Hunting flights within the forest are also made, and sometimes "still-hunting" from a lookout perch is employed. Birds make up much of the prey, ranging in size from warblers up to Red-legged Partridges and even a juvenile Little Bustard in one instance. Nests are also plundered for eggs or young – examples recorded include such diverse species as Purple Heron and Mistle Thrush. Lizards make up much of the prey in Spain, particularly the Ocellated Lizard. Mammal prey include rabbits, susliks (ground squirrels), red squirrels and voles. Records from the winter quarters are more fragmentary, but include various pigeons and domestic fowl, and a raid on the nest of a White-crowned Shrike. Like many birds in Africa, they are prepared to take termites on the wing when these are swarming.

Booted Eagles are normally encountered singly or in pairs. They are monogamous, though it is thought that the pair bond is only of seasonal duration, unlike that in the related Bonelli's Eagle. However, association with a previous nest site may often result in members of a pair remating in a subsequent season. Pairing apparently occurs soon after return to the breeding area in early spring. At this time, the Booted Eagle indulges in frequent and highly spectacular aerial displays. These may be performed by either male or female or both together. High circling over the nest site is common; at the height of ascent, the bird appears to hang motionless in the sky for a time, then descend in a long flat glide over perhaps ⅓ mile. Even more conspicuous is the "sky-dance" display, which is accompanied by shrill, melodious calls. It consists of a series of manoeuvres starting with high circling in tight spirals at heights up to

Opposite: A pale phase adult of this strongly migratory species.

The Booted Eagle mainly confines itself to forested country.

2,500 feet or more. On the last few circles, the bird throws itself from side to side, then dives with wings held close to the body only to climb steeply up once more, make a half loop, then dive again. The sequence may be repeated several times, for up to half an hour. The calls are given as the bird turns to dive from the half loop, and sometimes in other phases. The wings vibrate violently as they are opened to check each dive. Mock fighting and talon presentation also take place between members of a pair, and in the courtship flight, the pair fly together, the male positioned close above his mate.

Booted Eagles are strongly territorial, although in favorable habitat, nests may be very close together, with as little as 100-200 yards separating them. They defend their territory vigorously against intruders of their own or other species of birds of prey. When themselves mobbed by other birds, they may speed up, then execute a half roll to present the talons to their attackers. However, I have seen a Booted Eagle forced to flee in confusion by the attacks of a pair of Eleonora's Falcons, a raptor whose aerial prowess far exceeds their own. One form of territorial advertisement appears to be a prerogative of males of the pale color form. This consists simply of selecting a prominent perch, and sitting facing the sun, with the white breast displayed. If alarmed, it at once reverses its position to present the much less conspicuous upperparts to the intruder.

Although 1 or 2 alternative nests may be used, many territories are too small to permit many changes of site, and the same one may be used

A female shading its young from the sun.

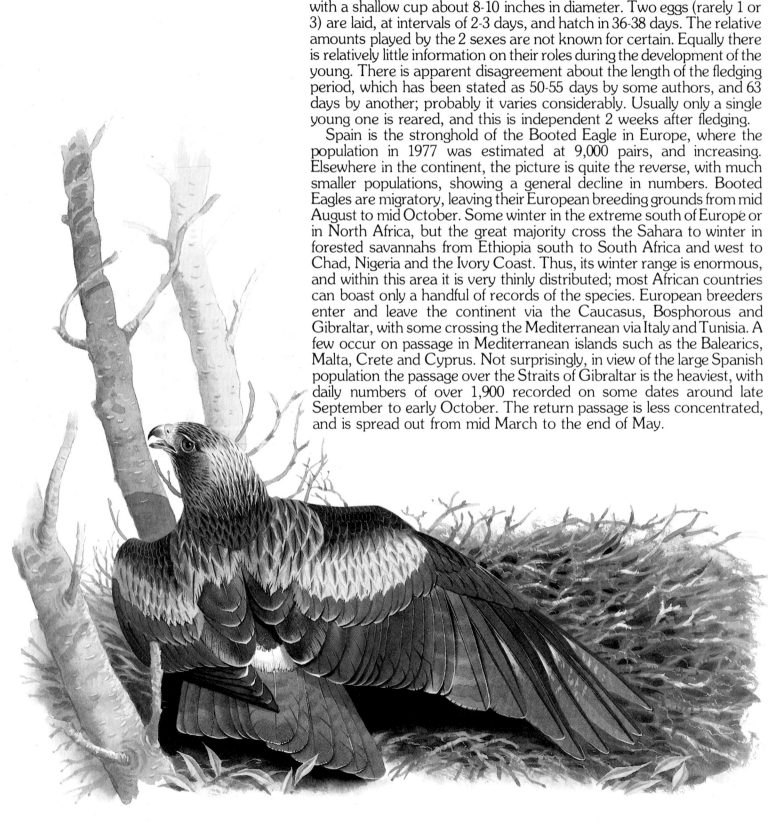

repeatedly, year after year. Rather flat in shape, the nest is made of branches, lined with green foliage and measures 3¼-4 feet in diameter, with a shallow cup about 8-10 inches in diameter. Two eggs (rarely 1 or 3) are laid, at intervals of 2-3 days, and hatch in 36-38 days. The relative amounts played by the 2 sexes are not known for certain. Equally there is relatively little information on their roles during the development of the young. There is apparent disagreement about the length of the fledging period, which has been stated as 50-55 days by some authors, and 63 days by another; probably it varies considerably. Usually only a single young one is reared, and this is independent 2 weeks after fledging.

Spain is the stronghold of the Booted Eagle in Europe, where the population in 1977 was estimated at 9,000 pairs, and increasing. Elsewhere in the continent, the picture is quite the reverse, with much smaller populations, showing a general decline in numbers. Booted Eagles are migratory, leaving their European breeding grounds from mid August to mid October. Some winter in the extreme south of Europe or in North Africa, but the great majority cross the Sahara to winter in forested savannahs from Ethiopia south to South Africa and west to Chad, Nigeria and the Ivory Coast. Thus, its winter range is enormous, and within this area it is very thinly distributed; most African countries can boast only a handful of records of the species. European breeders enter and leave the continent via the Caucasus, Bosphorous and Gibraltar, with some crossing the Mediterranean via Italy and Tunisia. A few occur on passage in Mediterranean islands such as the Balearics, Malta, Crete and Cyprus. Not surprisingly, in view of the large Spanish population the passage over the Straits of Gibraltar is the heaviest, with daily numbers of over 1,900 recorded on some dates around late September to early October. The return passage is less concentrated, and is spread out from mid March to the end of May.

HIERAETUS KIENERII

Adult

Young

In flight the adult's chestnut belly contrasts strongly with the white head and breast.

Following page: The handsome but little known Chestnut-bellied Hawk-Eagle. This eagle is usually seen over lowland forests or river valleys.

Though widely distributed, from India to the Philippines and Sulawesi, the Chestnut-bellied Hawk-Eagle occurs rather patchily and locally within its range, and is not at all well known. As it seems to depend ultimately on the fast-disappearing forests of Asia, its future must be considered insecure at best. It appears to be rather closely related to Ayres' Hawk-Eagle of Africa, but is more striking in appearance, with brighter coloring and a longer crest. Two races are recognized, that of India and Ceylon being larger and considerably paler above.

It seems to prefer lowland forest, below 4,000 feet, and is quite often seen along the valley of a large river, and sometimes over cleared areas. Part of its time is spent inconspicuously perched in the canopy, but it seems to hunt largely from soaring flight over the forest. When prey is sighted, it dives at high speed straight into the foliage, with wings almost folded. Birds are the usual prey, up to the size of pigeons or large kingfishers, and some small mammals are also taken.

Displays have not been described, but are unlikely to differ greatly from those of other hawk eagles, which include frequent vertical stoops. Its nests are built 80-100 feet up in forest trees. They are made of sticks, and lined with green leaves, and because they are used for many years, they become quite large structures, up to 4 feet across and 2 feet deep. Each pair usually has at least one alternative nest. The single egg is white, blotched with red-brown and gray. Both parents incubate, and are said to be very aggressive at the nest site.

Seen in the field, adults are distinguished from all other eagles by their unique color pattern. Immatures could be confused with the much commoner changeable Hawk-Eagle, Spizaetus cirrhatus, but have longer wings and a shorter tail. Seen overhead, the underwing appears white, with a dark rear edge, and a black patch at the wrist joint. No calls have been described for this species, which is evidently a very silent bird.

LOPHAETUS OCCIPITALIS

Bird watchers visiting East Africa are likely to see the Long-crested Eagle early in their tour, for it is often encountered by the roadside, perched on a tree or telegraph pole. Although it can be found in moist savannahs and riverine forest, it is more numerous around cultivated land where man's activities have attracted high populations of rodents. Its association with man in this way should be of benefit to both, but inevitably it is sometimes branded as a chicken thief – a reputation which it rarely justifies.

Seen perched, this species is easily recognized by the crest, which even the mottled immatures possess, though shorter. In flight overhead, it shows rather narrow wings with barred secondaries and a pale patch at the base of the primaries. This feature, combined with the dark body and boldly banded tail are sufficient to identify it.

Handsome though it is, the Long-crested Eagle is not a particularly powerful or rapacious species. It hunts mainly by watching from a perch, and catches its prey on the ground – mostly small mammals, varied with some lizards, small snakes and insects. A nesting pair range no more than about a mile from the breeding site, and use the same regular sequence of perches from day to day.

Long-crested eagles are noisy, with loud ringing calls. Long drawn out cries accompany the display flights which appear to consist mainly of soaring at about 330-500 feet, not involving spectacular aerobatics. It gives the display calls also while perched, usually near the nest. This is placed in a large tree, anywhere from 20 feet upwards, and usually

This eagle sometimes attends bush fires to capture small animals escaping the flames.

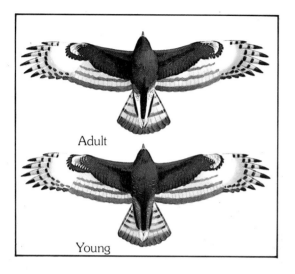

Dark body and strong barred tail
distinguish this eagle in flight.

towards the center of the tree where it is well shaded. Wild figs or eucalyptuses are frequently chosen. The nest is rather small, about 24 × 12 inches. Both sexes build or refurbish the nest, which may be used several years running. It is made of sticks and lined with green leaves.

Two eggs are usually laid, generally in the second half of the dry season. Incubation is by the female, who is fed by the male, but may occasionally spend short spells hunting for herself. The incubation period is not known. The male continues to provide most of the food for the first week or two after hatching, but by about 3 weeks, the female is bringing more prey than her mate. Some food is regurgitated into the nest, then fed to the young. Only one is usually reared successfully. This is feathered at 28 days, moves out onto branches from 45-50 days, and makes its first flight at about 55. The parents continue to feed it for 2 weeks or so after it has left, but it does not remain for long near the nest site.

The Long-crested Eagle can be seen in some cultivated areas attracted by high populations of rodents. Despite the impressive crest this is one of the less formidable eagles of Africa.

T. BOYER 80.

SPIZASTUR MELANOLEUCUS

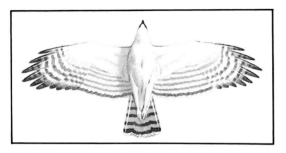

Short broad wings and pure white underparts are distinctive features in flight.

Opposite: This handsome eagle hunts birds and tree mammals in dense forest.

Although its pied plumage renders the Black-and-White Hawk Eagle extremely conspicuous, even in its habitat of rain forest, it is rarely seen. Ranging over most of the New World tropics, from southern Mexico to northern Argentina, it nevertheless appears to be very thinly distributed throughout this huge area. I am very lucky to have seen one in Panama in 1972, a country for which only 10 records are detailed in Wetmore's comprehensive regional work. Near the tiny town of El Real in Darien, I had just traversed the narrow surrounding zone of cattle grazing and secondary scrub to enter primary rain forest, when a movement in the canopy caught my eye. A large black and white raptor swept in through the foliage to perch on a high limb above the track, perched there for a few seconds, and then on sighting me, made off through the forest greenery as suddenly and mysteriously as it had appeared. Most sightings of the bird seem to be of this brief and unexpected nature, so it is no surprise that little is known of its habits and breeding biology.

In northern Argentina, the Black-and-White Hawk Eagle is found only along rivers, where cormorants and mergansers are said to be among its prey. Near Chepo, Panama, Wetmore records a bird dashing in through high forest to strike at Araçari toucans, while the bird I saw in Darien may have been attracted by Owl Monkeys nearby.

It is a very wry commentary on the priorities of past collectors that we know more about this bird's eggs than its nest, which has apparently never been described. The usual clutch is probably 2, and the eggs are cream-white, spotted with dark brown, lilac and light brown.

At rest, the Black-and-White Hawk Eagle adopts an upright, flat-headed, thoroughly aquiline pose, and its plumage pattern renders it unmistakable. In flight, its outline is reminiscent of a Buteo (buzzard). Immatures resemble the adult, but have white edgings on the wing coverts, and an extra bar on the tail. Its closest relatives are probably the Black and the Barred Hawk Eagles, genus Spizaetus.

SPIZAETUS ORNATUS

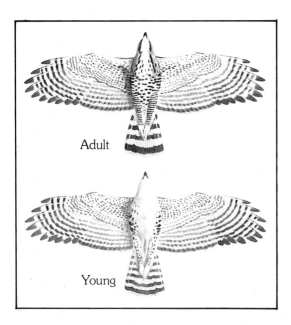

Adult

Young

Short broad wings and long barred tail create the appearance of a giant Goshawk in flight.

This eagle lives in deep tropical American forests.

Resplendent in black, white and rufous, with a long mobile crest, this is arguably South America's most handsome raptor. Striking and widely distributed though it is, however, its habits are not at all well known. It inhabits rain forest, but prefers areas with some open ground, and apparently hunts mainly from lookout perches at medium heights. Seen on one of these perches it has a rather thickset, buzzard-like stance; passing overhead, its tail appears long and broad, the wings short and rounded. Medium or large birds appear to form its prey, varied with some arboreal mammals, such as raccoons and monkeys. There is a record of one killing and eating a black vulture which had come to the carcase of a monkey – possibly a previous kill of the eagle. Wetmore states that it is said to feed on reptiles, and he saw one capture a Ringed Kingfisher.

Ornate Hawk Eagles are most frequently seen around the breeding season, when they indulge in aerial displays, often soaring on flat wings, or spiraling upwards with wing flaps. Pairs are frequently seen soaring together, but the female (presumably) may eventually perch while the male performs an undulating display consisting of alternating shallow dives and climbs, accompanied by loud calling – a high pitched scream. Sometimes aerial loops are performed, and at all times, the rufous neck coloring stands out.

Two nests have been reported. One, in Chiapas, was found after the tree was felled, the female having spent much time at it previously. Its only contents were prey remains. Another, in Panama, was sited 100 feet high in a fork of a tall tree leaning over a ravine. Adults visited it frequently during the dry season, and by the wet (late April to May) a young bird was often visible from the ground. Visits by adults were marked by loud vocalization, the adults calling "whur wheep" or similar sounds and the young birds contributing cheeping sounds.

Opposite: The crest is raised when excited or alarmed.

SPIZAETUS BARTELSI

With an area about that of England, but twice the human population, Java is one of the most densely inhabited areas of the world. Despite this, some forest and wilderness survives, mostly on the slopes of the volcanic mountain chain which forms the spine of the island. This remnant provides the habitat of the rare and little-known Java Hawk Eagle, but is gradually shrinking, and while this continues, the future of this impressive bird of prey must remain in the balance.

In size, this species lies between the large Mountain Hawk-Eagle of continental Asia and Wallace's Hawk-Eagle of Malaysia. In plumage it resembles the former, but the neighboring islands are occupied by the quite distinct Blyth's Hawk-Eagle, so there seems little doubt that the Javan bird is truly a distinct species. Sadly, there is practically no information available on its life and habits. Even its eggs are undescribed, often one of the first pieces of information to be documented about a bird! It can only be hoped that it will survive long enough for the gaps to be filled, and that the mystery which surrounds it will not also prove its downfall.

It is uncertain how many pairs of this little known eagle survive.

The habitat of forested mountains has been drastically reduced during the last century.

31 CROWNED EAGLE

STEPHANOAETUS CORONATUS

Though only two-thirds the weight of the Martial Eagle, and with but a modest wing span, the Crowned Eagle is Africa's most powerful species, with exceptionally well developed legs and feet, and enormous hind talons. These structural features give the clue to its way of life; the Crowned Eagle is a species of forest or well-timbered areas, which hunts mainly by waiting and watching, from a vantage point, taking prey by dropping on it from above or after a swift chase. The relatively short wings permit agile flight through a network of branches and foliage, and the huge talons can deal quickly with prey up to the size of small antelopes to repay lengthy vigils in ambush. The Crowned Eagle is thus, roughly, Africa's equivalent to the Harpy Eagle of South America, or the Monkey-eating Eagle of the Philippines, though not closely related to either. It provides an interesting contrast to other large, but more aerial species such as the Martial Eagle or Black Eagle; seeking their quarry in long bouts of soaring, very large legs and feet would be an aerodynamic liability to them, but instead they have wing area developed to a maximum. It may be supposed that these birds take smaller prey on average, but capture them more frequently; however, this would be to reason ahead of the established facts, and a vast amount of fieldwork is still needed before even such basic hypotheses can be sustained or refuted.

The crown feathers are valuable ornaments among some African peoples.

Seen in flight, the Crowned Eagle looks somewhat like an enormous Goshawk, with short broad wings heavily barred below, and long barred tail. Tail length and barring is particularly important in the case of immatures, which otherwise resemble those of the Martial Eagle; in the case of adults, the rich chestnut under wing coverts and barred underparts provide additional diagnostic features. According to Brown and Amadon, males may be known from females in flight by their more rapid wing beats. Another interesting property of the bird's flight, though scarcely useful as a field character, is its silence. Though soundless flight is more usually associated with owls, Peter Steyn testifies to the remarkably noiseless arrival of Crowned Eagles at the nests he watched. Doubtless this ability is of great value to the bird as it swoops down on an intended victim.

In the past it has been supposed that monkeys formed the bulk of the Crowned Eagle's diet. More recent studies indicate that these are only a minor item of the bird's diet, except perhaps in heavily forested areas. Much commoner prey are small antelopes and victims whose relatively large size testifies to the great power of the Crowned Eagle's legs and feet. Mammals form the great bulk of the prey, including a few carnivores such as mongooses and domestic cats. Apart from the latter, however, man's livestock appear rarely, if ever, to be harmed. Smaller items sometimes taken include rats, monitor lizards and large snakes.

Hunting perches are often chosen to overlook a waterhole or forest clearing, and they are occupied especially during morning or evening, when movements of mammals are at a peak. Once a kill has been made, the Crowned Eagle can rise nearly vertically with it from the ground to dismember it at a tree perch. It is believed to cache some pieces of prey in trees for later consumption; also the members of a pair feed freely on each other's kills. A certain amount of prey is taken in the treetops, as well as on the ground, and it has been credited with uttering a soft whistle to lure monkeys into easy range. The tables can be sometimes

Hyraxes, Dik-diks and Colobus monkeys are regular prey.

Opposite: This handsome eagle is Africa's most powerful species.

turned, however, for at one nest watched by Leslie Brown, a Syke's Monkey was seen deliberately baiting a female Crowned Eagle brooding a small young one, snatching at the bird and bounding over it, regardless of the Eagle's threatening behavior.

The Crowned Eagle is a noisy species, and this is especially the case during the male's display flights. These consist largely of a switchback series of dives and ascents at a great height, with a few wingbeats at the top of each climb. Coinciding with the wingbeats, the head is thrown back, and a high-pitched "Kewee-kewee-kewee" is uttered, sometimes in prolonged bursts of up to half a minute. The female has a lower pitched call uttered both while perched, and during mutual display flights involving both members of the pair. When bringing prey to the young, either sex may use a shrill "quee-quee-quee-quee", to which the eaglet may respond with a similar cry. Males have higher pitched voices than females, and those of young birds are higher still.

We now have a detailed knowledge of the Crowned Eagle's breeding biology, thanks mainly to the extensive observations of Leslie Brown. Unlike many eagles, a pair usually have only one nest, sited in a large forest tree anywhere from 40-150 feet high. Made of sticks, with a lining of green branches, it is used over a long period of time by successive birds. Building is carried out by both sexes, though the female takes a larger share. Long established nests may be approximately 6 feet across, and 10 feet deep.

The nest is the usual site of mating, which is often preceded by a display in which the male runs around the female with wings raised to show their striking chestnut linings and barring. The clutch which eventually results consists of 1-2 eggs, plain white, or with a few reddish brown marks. Dates of laying vary widely over Africa as a whole, but for the most part fall between July and October.

Usually both parents share the duties of incubation, which lasts 49 days, and caring for the young, though in some cases the former duty is performed only by the female, with the male bringing food. Her behavior when he arrives with prey seems ungracious to human eyes, as she is liable to snatch it from him and "mantle" over it aggressively with half raised wings. Peter Steyn notes that this is the only eagle in his experience in which the female exhibits this behaviour so strongly, but in some pairs, nevertheless, roles may be reversed for a time with the female bringing meals to an incubating male. The rate of delivery to a sitting bird is a kill once every 3-5 days.

The eaglets become active soon after hatching and in broods of 2, the weaker succumbing to the stronger quite early in development. The female parent takes the greater share of tending the young at first, while the male doubles his hunting rate. While the eaglet is still small, the female prepares food for it carefully; Peter Steyn notes that pieces of liver were apparently specially selected from a dassie (hyrax) for one downy young one. Nevertheless, the young eagle rapidly learns to feed itself and by 60 days old its mother has largely relinquished the nest and thereafter concentrates on hunting, bringing even more prey than the male. In the final stages of her duties at the nest, the female moves about in its vicinity, frequently bringing green sprays of foliage to add to its lining. During this period also, she is dangerously aggressive, and will strike a human intruder readily, sometimes inflicting a gash with her

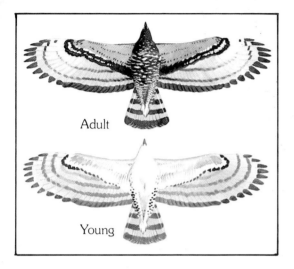

The Crowned Eagle shows the short winged characteristics of forest species and inhabits forest or open woodland.

formidable talons. Even in captivity, Crowned Eagles are not to be trifled with, and have been known to injure their owners.

The development of the young one is well documented. First feathers make their appearance at about 40 days, the crest at about 60, and by 76 days there is a complete covering of feathers. The hind claw grows rapidly, and quite often gets caught in the nest material, causing the young birds to stumble – an irritation which sometimes befalls its parents as well. From 45-50 days, wing flapping exercises begin, becoming more intensive after about 70 days. The young leaves the nest at about 110 days, often (especially males) climbing about on branches before making the first flight of 50-330 feet. In the Kenyan birds studied by Leslie Brown, the young one remained in the neighborhood of the nest from 9 months to nearly a year after making its first flight, and during that time continued to be fed at 3-5 day intervals. Occasionally it may kill for itself during that time, the earliest recorded case being 61 days after leaving the nest, yet it continues to beg for food with insistent loud calls whenever an adult appears. The eventual break, interestingly, seems to be due more to the young bird's increasing independence than to any neglect by the parents – a reversal of the situation found in many birds of prey. As a result of this very long period of dependence, these eagles were only able to breed every other year. However, at a nest studied in Natal, the parents managed to rear young in several successive years, chasing away the previous year's offspring when the new breeding cycle started.

The Crowned Eagle seems still to be fairly common in good habitat throughout Africa. The chief dangers to its survival lie in the reduction of that habitat, and in the numbers of its prey species, especially hyraxes. Peter Steyn notes that in areas of the Matopos in Zimbabwe where human hunting pressure has severely reduced the hyrax population, the breeding success of Black Eagles (also dependent on them) has been adversely affected, and the same may well be true of Crowned Eagles.

OROAETUS ISIDORI

Also known as the Black and Chestnut Eagle, this impressive bird is closely related to the Ornate Hawk-Eagle. It differs in its larger size and more powerful build, seemingly a rough ecological counterpart on mountain slopes to the Harpy and Crested Eagles of flatter forests. Unlike all of these, however, it has relatively long wings, indicating that much of its time searching for prey is spent in the air, and victims are seized from the top of the forest canopy. Were it to dash in among the branches like a Harpy Eagle, long wings would be a hindrance. Its typical habitat is the subtropical or temperate forest of the Andes up to approximately 9,000 feet, though locally it may occur down to sea level. Steep gorges and ravines clothed with oaks and silver-leaved Cecropias are characteristic of this country, but despite the difficult terrain, deforestation is proceeding rapidly. Thinly distributed even in the best habitat, Isidor's Eagle seems certain to dwindle rapidly in numbers as this continues.

Our knowledge of the bird's prey is derived to a large extent from the accounts of Indians living in the same areas. Churucos or woolly monkeys, squirrels, sloths, porcupines and raccoons are among the variety of tree living mammals captured. Birds include guans, and occasionally poultry. The latter, found around mountain villages, appear mainly to be taken by immature birds.

Oaks seem to be preferred for nesting, and also for providing the raw material for the nest itself. Live branches are mainly used, obtained by plunging and seizing one in passing, so that momentum aids the bird in breaking it off. The nest is a large one, placed at least 65 feet up in a tree, and frequently overhanging a gorge. East facing slopes are preferred, as these receive the benefit of the early morning sun, which is usually obliterated by cloud as the day progresses. One egg is believed to be the usual clutch, and only a single egg appears ever to have been described; it was white, washed and spotted with chocolate. Exact incubation times are not known, but an egg laid in April at one nest was hatched in May, and in July, the young one was still in the nest, not ready to leave. When feeding the eaglet, the male appears to do most of the hunting, bringing in mainly squirrels until the young are 8 weeks old. He drops in swiftly, with half closed wings, uttering a loud "pee-ee-eeo," to which the female may respond with a similar cry. Having left his prey, he retires to a nearby perch. Usually, the female then feeds it to the young one, but in her absence, the male may do so. The immature bird can fly when 4 months old, but lives for a further 6 months or so in the locality of the nest. Apart from the greeting call, a "Kee-kee-kee" is used to warn the young of danger, and a softer version of this is occasionally heard as a communication note.

Juvenile birds are much paler than adults, with light feather edgings on the upper parts, and no chestnut below. Their crest feathers, however, are almost as long as those of mature birds. The eye is blue-gray at first, becoming yellow around 3 months of age.

Young birds could be confused with those of Hawk Eagles, but Isidor's can always be identified by the habitat in which it occurs.

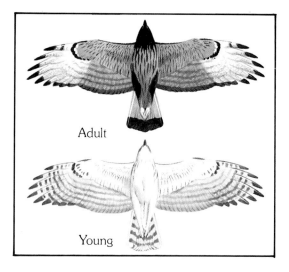

Adult

Young

A contrasting pattern of black and white and chestnut unlike any other bird of prey identifies this eagle.

Opposite: Handsomely crested this eagle takes the place of the Harpy and Guyana Eagles at higher altitudes.

Isidor's Eagle inhabits the densely forested Andean valleys.

T. BOYER 81.

33 MARTIAL EAGLE

POLEMAETUS BELLICOSUS

Opposite: Africa's largest eagle, the Martial hunts large prey in open country.

Immature birds lack the dark head and breast of the adult.

Africa's largest eagle, the Martial's impressive size is matched by its striking plumage. Large females may have a wingspan of 8 feet, and weigh over 13 lbs. Though equipped with less powerful – but still formidable – talons than the Crowned Eagle, its wings are considerably longer, reflecting its much more aerial way of life. Not only does the Martial Eagle seek its prey from soaring flight, but it spends much of its day on the wing even when not actually hunting. Early morning or late evening offer the best chance of seeing a Martial Eagle perched, other than at the nest site. The rest of the time it is most likely to be seen overhead, often at immense height, when the contrast of dark wings and head with pale body is characteristic. Immature birds could conceivably be confused with immatures of the Crowned Eagle, but are much more narrowly and indistinctly barred on wings and tail, and of course have quite a different flight outline.

The Martial Eagle inhabits more open country than the Crowned – savannah or bushveldt areas, usually with scattered thorn trees. The home range of a pair may form 50 sq miles of such country, and they wander extensively within it. Young birds may move further; a fledgling ringed by Peter Steyn in Rhodesia was recovered 10 months later 40 miles northwest of the nest site. Within their home range, it seems that a pair usually exploit one area for several days in succession and then move on.

Prey are often spotted from a considerable distance, and attacked by a long slanting stoop at high speed – a manoeuvre which usually takes the victim completely by surprise. The Martial Eagle's diet usually includes a large proportion of birds – up to 80 per cent in some areas. These are predominantly medium or large species, such as francolins, guinea fowl and bustards; even European Stork is recorded. Mammals most frequently taken are hyraxes and dik-dik (small antelopes). Monkeys figure in the menu, as well as the young of some larger animals such as Impala, and domestic sheep or goats. Some of the mammals eaten are themselves carnivores, such as mongooses and even serval cat and jackal. Though attacks on lambs, kid and poultry are less frequent than some farmers claim, they occur often enough to place the bird at high risk of being shot in some areas. This risk, and increasing human pressure on the environment generally are the principal dangers threatening the Martial Eagle's future.

Adult

Young

Long barred wings and black head and breast are field marks in flight.

The dry season in African savannahs is a good time for hunting since less shelter is available for prey. The Martial seeks its victim whilst soaring at great height over the bush.

Display flights do not appear to be highly developed in this species. There is a display call, rendered "klee-klee-klee-klooee-klooee-kuleee" given either while soaring or perched, which carries for a long distance, but aerobatics comparable with those of other eagles have not been recorded. Martial Eagles build typical large eagle nests of sticks up to 1¼ inches in diameter, with a lining of green leaves, and site them in trees of African beech, from 20-85 feet above the ground. General accounts suggest that just 1 or 2 nests are used by a pair, but Steyn's own experience has been different. Regardless of success or failure in any one year, they constructed new nests or unexpectedly reused old ones; over 10 years, he located seven different nests within a home range. One common factor emerged, however; most of the nests were sited in the neck of a valley, probably because air currents on the slope assisted

them in their comings and goings. Construction or repair of the nest seems to be done chiefly by the female, with the male occasionally bringing sticks. A single egg only is normally laid, white or pale greenish blue in ground colour with brown and gray markings. Laying dates show no clear correlation with seasons.

Incubation apparently lasts between 44-51 days, and is mainly by the female, although the male has sometimes been seen to brood the eggs. Peter Steyn has also recorded a male brooding the young – one of the few such cases in his extensive experience of eagles, though he notes that the bird seemed ill at ease first before settling on the young one. The eaglet shows its first feathers at 32 days, is fairly well covered by them at 50 days, and completely feathered at 70 days. It is fed by its parents up to 60 days, and from then on has to prepare its own meals from the prey brought to it.

About 100 days is usually regarded as the fledging period, but a nestling was observed, flying well, at 75 days in response to the nesting site being climbed. This young bird was ringed and later recovered; it

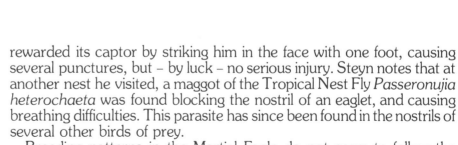

rewarded its captor by striking him in the face with one foot, causing several punctures, but – by luck – no serious injury. Steyn notes that at another nest he visited, a maggot of the Tropical Nest Fly *Passeronujia heterochaeta* was found blocking the nostril of an eaglet, and causing breathing difficulties. This parasite has since been found in the nostrils of several other birds of prey.

Breeding patterns in the Martial Eagle do not seem to follow the regular cycle seen in some African Eagles, such as the Crowned Eagle. Apparently breeding may take place several years in succession, followed by a number of non-breeding years. Leslie Brown records 31 breeding attempts in Kenya, from which 18 eggs were laid, and 13 young reared. The rate of reproduction suggested by this would indicate an average length of life of some 12-14 years in the wild. As with other large eagles, this low rate of replacement renders it very vulnerable to the effects of persecution.

MAPS

These maps are designed to show in a quick and simple way the areas of the world in which each species can be seen. For clarity, we have not attempted to show the ranges occupied by different races, or to distinguish breeding and winter ranges (which often overlap). The former can be found from the standard reference works such as *Eagles, Hawks and Falcons of the World*, by Leslie Brown and Dean Amadon, while movements within the range are explained in the text.

BALD EAGLE

Haliaeetus leucocephalus

North America

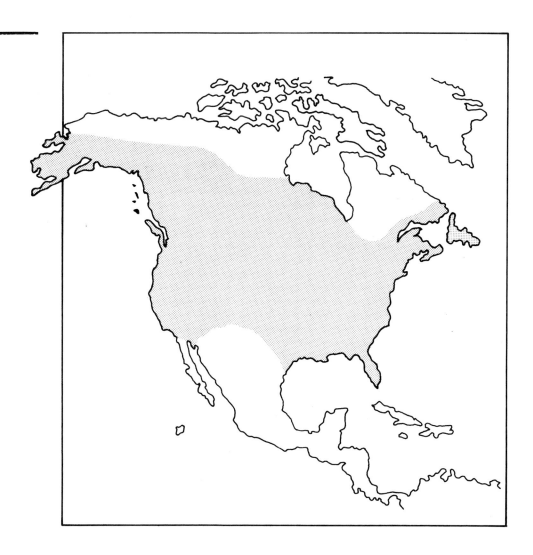

PALLAS'S FISH EAGLE

Haliaeetus leucoryphus

Central Asia

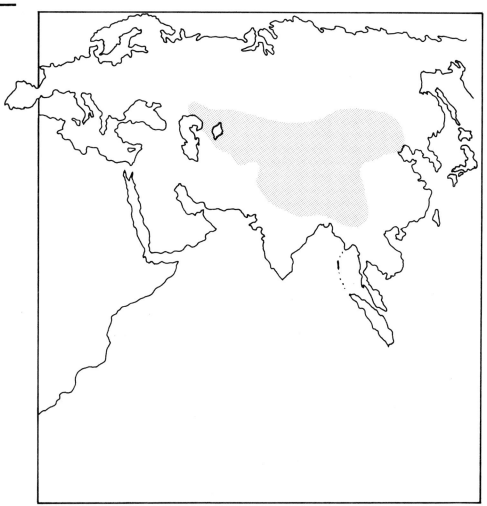

3 AFRICAN FISH EAGLE

Haliaeetus vocifer

Africa

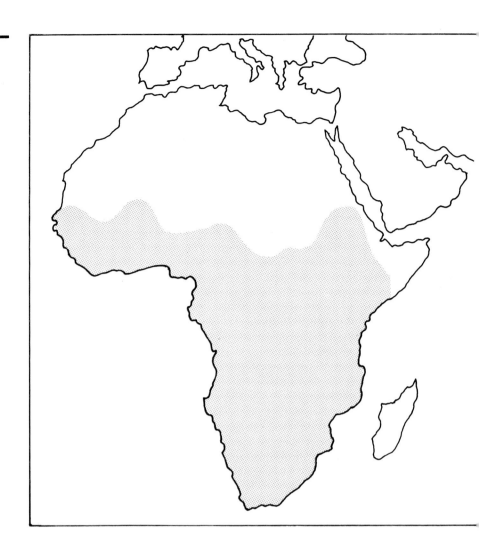

4 WHITE-BELLIED SEA EAGLE

Haliaeetus leucogaster

South-East Asia
Philippines
Indonesia
Malaysia
New Guinea
Australia

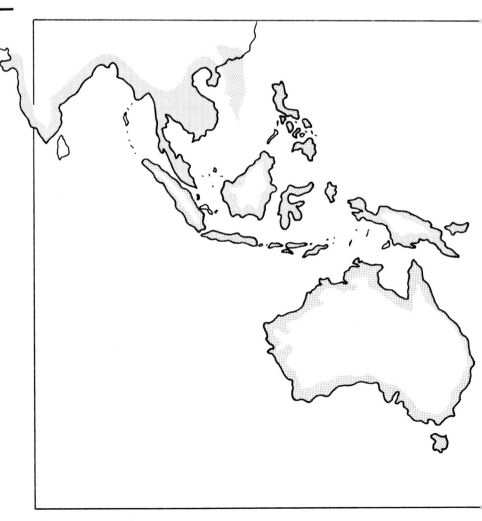

5 WHITE-TAILED SEA EAGLE

Haliaeetus albicilla

Russia/Eastern Europe

6 STELLER'S SEA EAGLE

Haliaeetus pelagicus

North-East Russia
(Manchurian Peninsula)

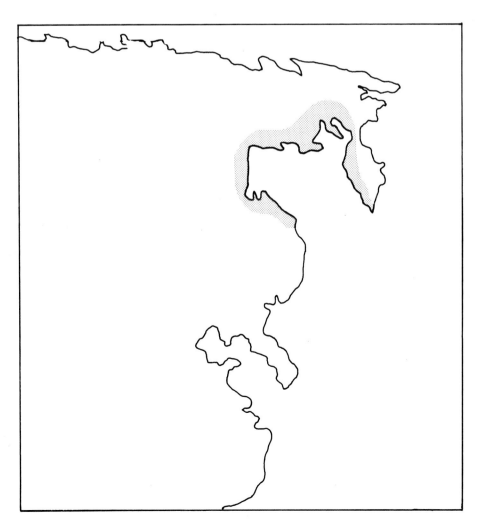

7 SHORT-TOED EAGLE

Circaetus gallicus

Central Africa/India/
Mediterrean/Spain

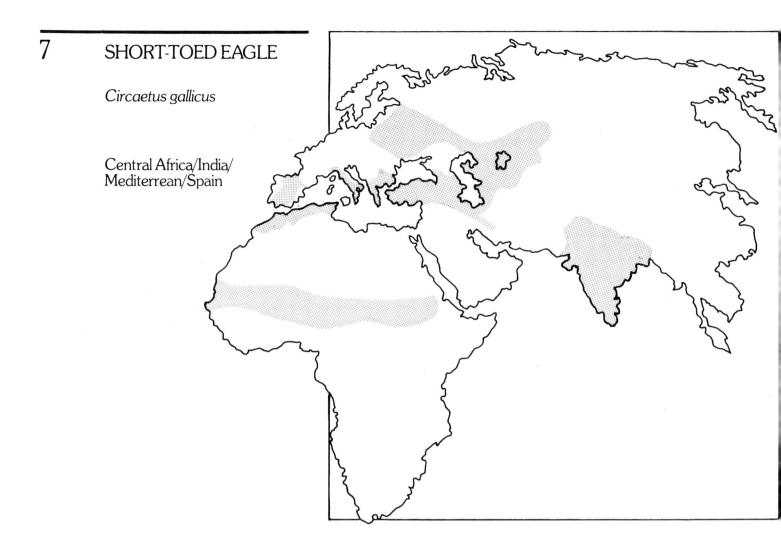

8 BATELEUR

& *Terathopius ecaudatus*

11 MADAGASCAR
SERPENT EAGLE

Eutriorchis astur

Africa & Madagascar

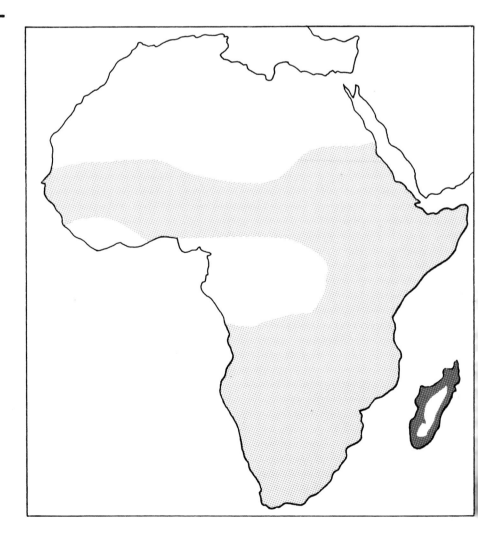

9 CRESTED SERPENT EAGLE

Spilornis cheela

South East Asia/
Indonesia/Malaysia

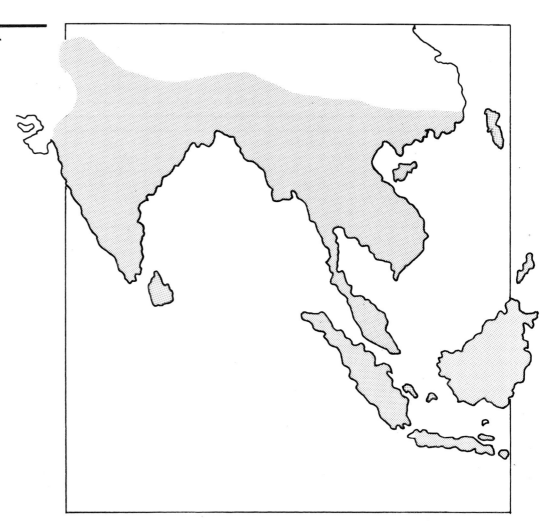

10 CELEBES SERPENT EAGLE

Spilornis rufipectus

Sulawesi
(Celebes & Sula Islands)

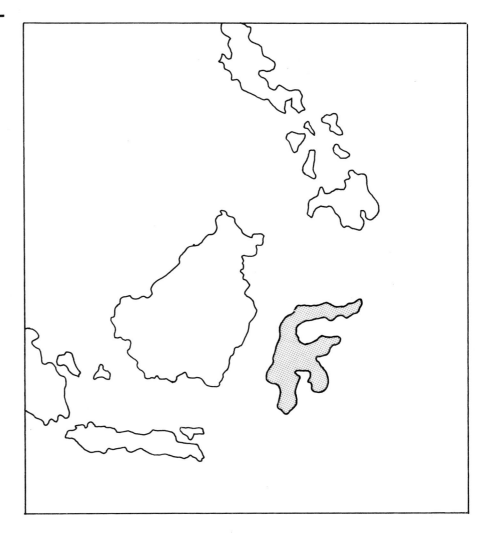

12 GUYANA CRESTED EAGLE

Morphnus guianensis

South America

13 HARPY EAGLE

Harpia harpyja

South America

14 NEW GUINEA EAGLE

Harpyopsis novaeguineae

New Guinea

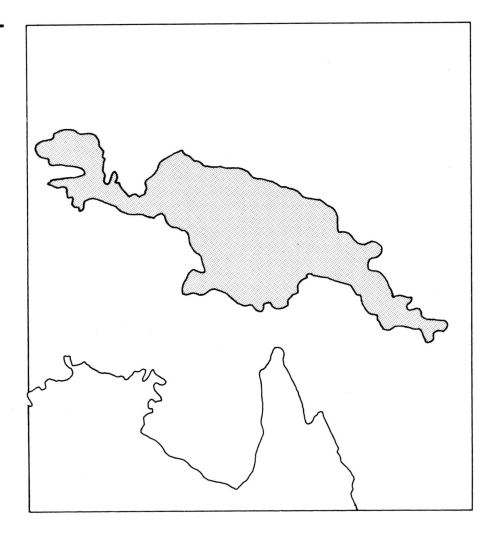

15 PHILIPPINE EAGLE

Pithecophaga jefferyi

Philippines

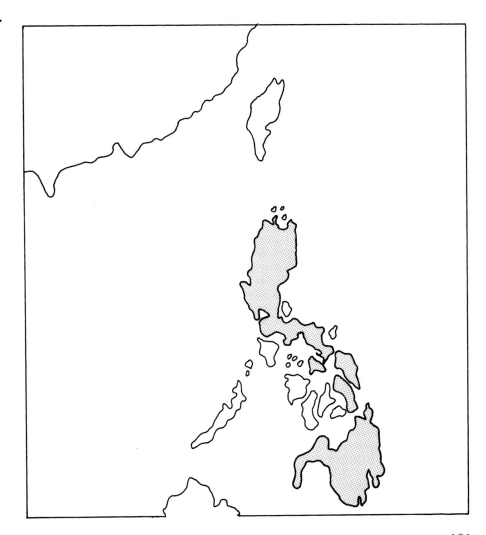

16 INDIAN BLACK EAGLE

Ictinaetus malayensis

South-East Asia/
Indonesia/Malaysia

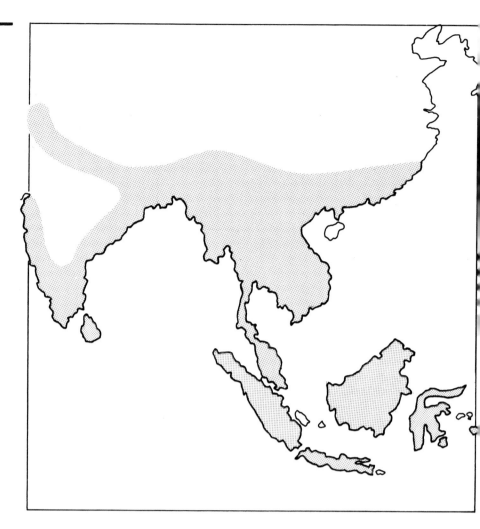

17 SPOTTED EAGLE

Aquila clanga

Eastern Europe/
Central Asia/India

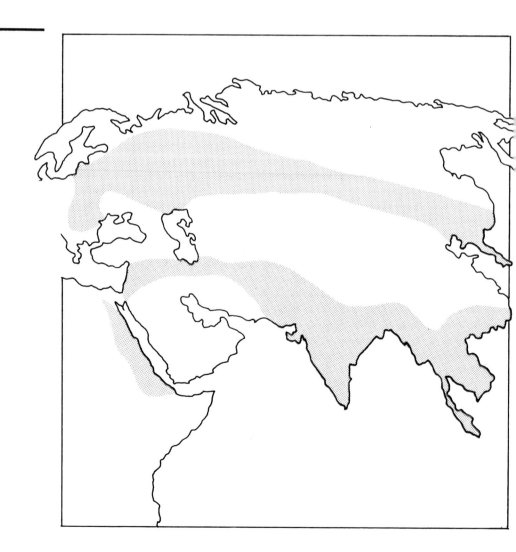

18 STEPPE EAGLE

Aquila rapax

Central Asia/
India/Africa

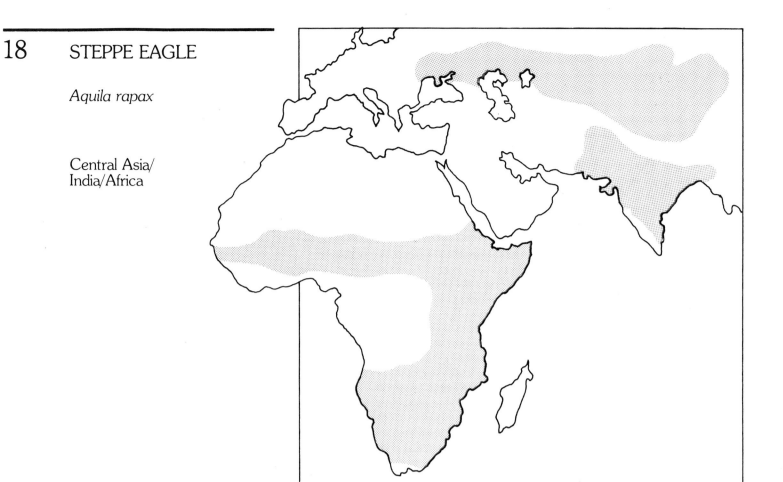

19 IMPERIAL EAGLE

Aquila heliaca

South-Eastern Europe

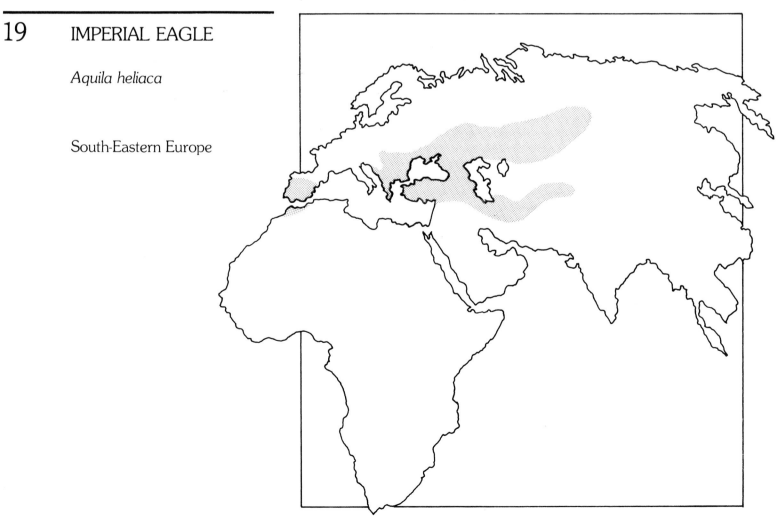

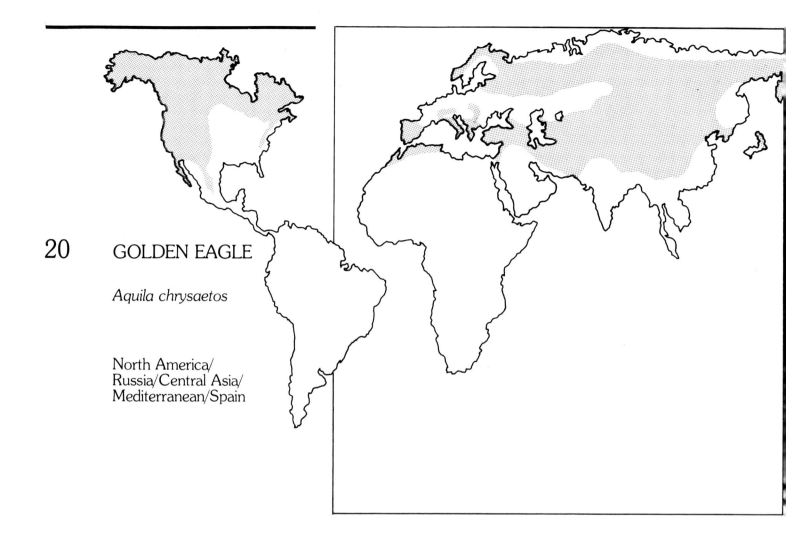

20 GOLDEN EAGLE

Aquila chrysaetos

North America/
Russia/Central Asia/
Mediterranean/Spain

21 WEDGE-TAILED EAGLE

Aquila audax

New Guinea/
Australia

22 GURNEY'S EAGLE

Aquila gurneyi

New Guinea

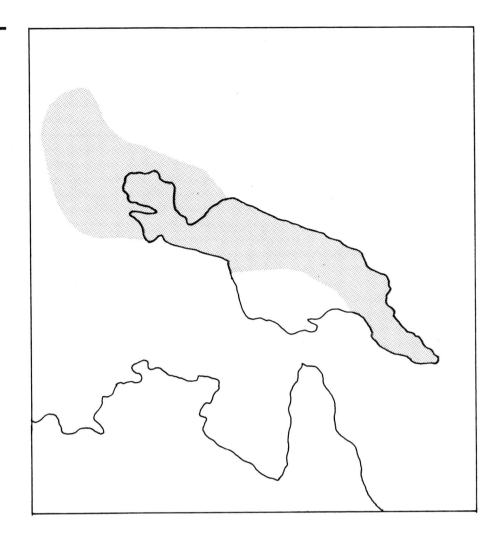

23 BLACK EAGLE

Aquila verreauxi

Africa

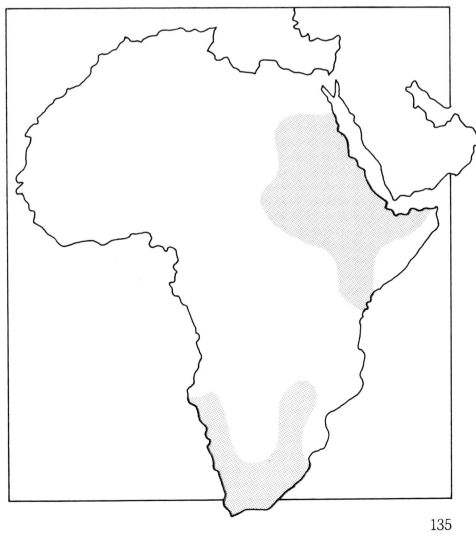

24 BONELLI'S EAGLE

Hieraetus fasciatus

Spain/Africa/India/
South-East Asia

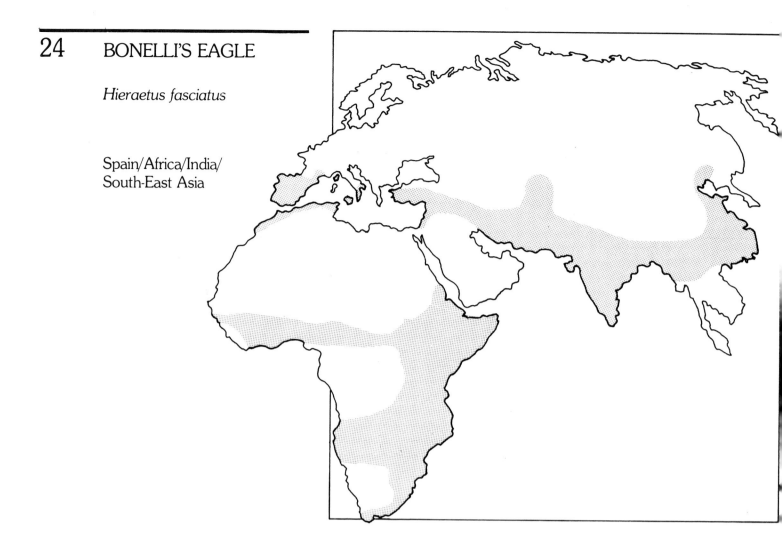

25 BOOTED EAGLE

Hieraetus pennatus

Spain/Mediterranean/Africa
India/Burma

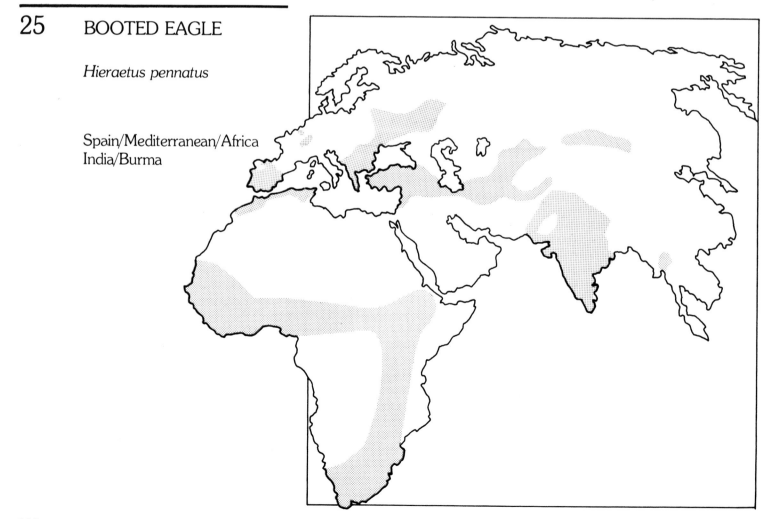

26 CHESTNUT-BELLIED HAWK EAGLE

Hieraetus kienerii

Sri Lanka/West India/
Thailand/Cambodia/
Indonesia/Malaysia

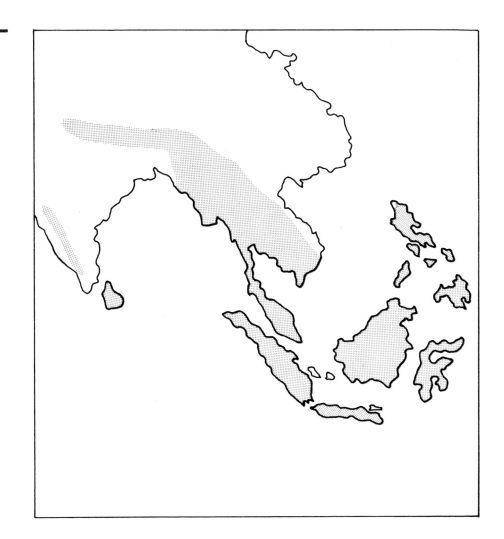

27 LONG-CRESTED EAGLE

Lophaetus occipitalis

Central Africa

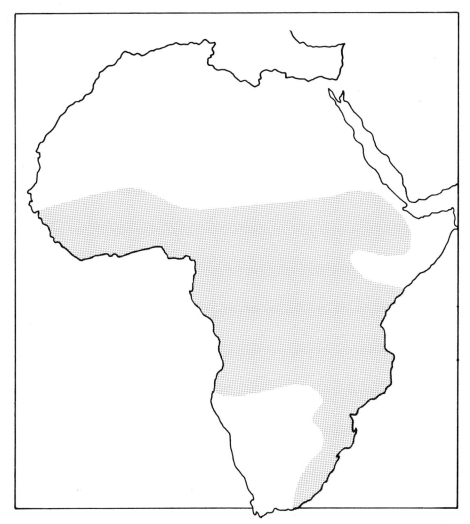

28 BLACK AND WHITE HAWK-EAGLE

Spizastur melanoleucus

South America

29 ORNATE HAWK EAGLE

Spizaetus ornatus

South America

30 JAVA HAWK-EAGLE

Spizaetus bartelsi

Indonesia

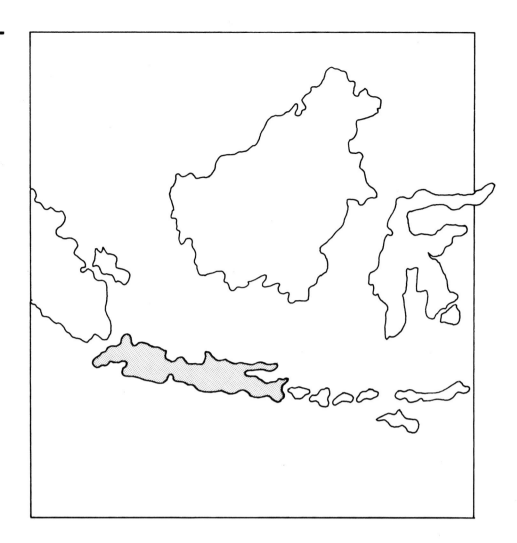

31 CROWNED EAGLE

Stephanoaetus coronatus

Central Africa

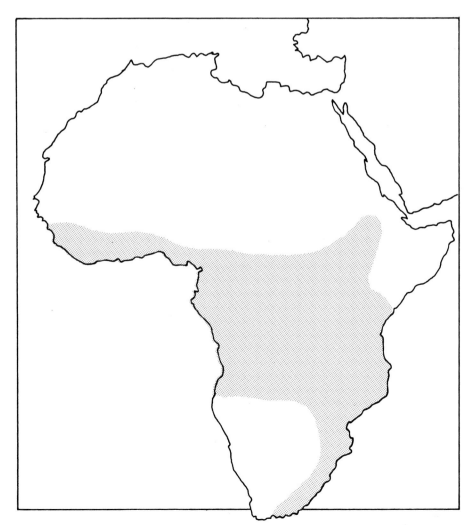

32 ISIDOR'S EAGLE

Oroaetus isidori

Western South America

33 MARTIAL EAGLE

Polemaetus bellicosus

Central Africa

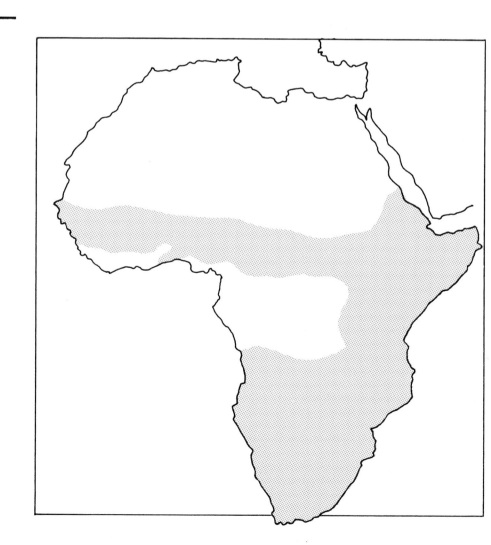